AT WHAT COST?

The economics of Gy
Traveller encampmenь

Rachel Morris and Luke Clements

The POLICY
P ~ P
PRESS

First published in Great Britain in September 2002 by

The Policy Press
34 Tyndall's Park Road
Bristol BS8 1PY
UK

Tel +44 (0)117 954 6800
Fax +44 (0)117 973 7308
e-mail tpp@bristol.ac.uk
www.policypress.org.uk

British Library Cataloguing in Publication Data

A catalogue record for this book is available from the British Library

ISBN 1 86134 423 6

Rachel Morris is Coordinator and **Luke Clements** is Co-Director, both at the Traveller Law Research Unit, Cardiff Law School.

Cover design by Qube Design Associates, Bristol.

Cover photographs by Taff, a Traveller himself for 15 years. The front cover photograph was taken during the British floods of Spring 2001, which affected encampments and sites of Travelling People as well as people in houses. The picture is not intended to represent a typical 'unauthorised encampment'.

Printed and bound in Great Britain by Henry Ling Limited, at the Dorset Press, Dorchester DT1 1HD.

Contents

List of tables

Preface

This report on research into the costs of unauthorised encampments is structured as follows:

- An outline of how the current law and policy relating to encampments in the United Kingdom was conceived and formulated, to set out clearly the background to these matters.
- The findings of the Traveller Law Research Unit (TLRU) as to the costs of such encampments and some of the issues raised by them.
- The Best Value regime, and other important and recent major legislative changes that may play a part in spending and policy related to encampments in the future; described and analysed in the context of related costs.

It is hoped that this research may assist with broadening views about who encampments concern, and with the process of developing approaches to encampments that are lawful, fair, balanced and practical. This book is intended for use by:

- Local authorities, police services and others involved with managing encampments: to aid them in looking 'laterally' at the issues as the government suggests and in the development of best practice; and to inform them as to how the cross-cutting issues engendered by new legislation might affect and assist them.
- Travelling People and those who provide services to them: to provide information as to the possible effects of current law and policy around encampments and other legislative developments.
- Central government: to assist the Office of the Deputy Prime Minister, the Home Office, the Audit Commission, and perhaps other agencies such as the Social Exclusion (Cabinet Office) and Inclusion (Scotland) Units, with their policy development in this area.
- The many students and staff members at all levels of the education system and in other fields who are themselves conducting research into issues of Best Value and/or those affecting Travelling People: this research makes a tentative step towards diminishing the lack of practical data and provides useful background material on current law and policy.
- Those who only see unauthorised encampments as a 'problem': acknowledging that they can be indeed, but that this is a complex issue requiring a wider understanding.

Acknowledgements

The Traveller Law Research Unit wishes to thank:

- Stephen Pittam and the Joseph Rowntree Charitable Trust for encouragement and financial assistance.
- Cardiff Law School for ongoing infrastructure support.
- All of those local authorities who took the time and trouble to respond to the research.
- The TLRU Advisory Group: Susan Alexander, Friends, Families and Travellers; Lord Avebury; Anne Bagehot, Gypsy Council for Education, Culture, Welfare and Civil Rights; Sandra Clay, Cardiff Traveller Education Service; Kay Beard and Sylvia Dunn, National Association of Gypsy Women; Eli Frankham, National Romani Rights Association; Terry Green; Hester Hedges; Mary Lee; Yvonne MacNamara, Irish Travellers' Project; Peter Mercer, East Anglian Gypsy Council; Tim Wilson, Cardiff Gypsy Sites Group.
- The Travelling People who gave their views on the costs to them of unauthorised encampments.
- The Traveller Section of Save the Children Fund Scotland, especially Michelle Lloyd, for comments and contributions.
- Bill Forrester, Kent County Council and Nick Payne, West Devon Borough Council, for their assistance in piloting the questionnaire and providing other information.
- Howard Davies and Janet Read at the University of Warwick.
- David Ayre, Environmental Services Directorate, Dorset County Council.
- Members of the Association of Chief Police Officers for opinions and information.
- Delegates to the TLRU seminar on Best Value and Unauthorised Encampments, London, July 2000.
- Colin Clark, Department of Social Policy, University of Newcastle.

List of acronyms

ACERT — Advisory Council for the Education of Romany and other Travellers

ACPO — Association of Chief Police Officers

AONB — Area of Outstanding Natural Beauty

BVPIs — Best Value Performance Indicators

BVPPs — Best Value Performance Plans

CC(s) — County council(s)

CCT — Compulsory Competitive Tendering

CIEH — Chartered Institute of Environmental Health

CJPOA — 1994 Criminal Justice and Public Order Act

CRE — Commission for Racial Equality

CRR — Community and Race Relations

CSA — 1968 Caravan Sites Act

DC(s) — District councils

DETR — Department of the Environment, Transport and the Regions (1997-2001)

DTLR — Department for Transport, Local Government and the Regions (2001-2002)

DoE — Department of the Environment (until 1997)

ECHR — European Convention on Human Rights

EO — Employers' Organisation for Local Government

FFT — Friends, Families and Travellers

HMIC	Her Majesty's Inspectorate of Constabulary
HMSO	Her Majesty's Stationery Office
HO	Home Office
HRA	1998 Human Rights Act
IDeA	Improvement and Development Agency for local government
LA(s)	Local authority(ies)
LBC(s)	London borough council(s)
LGA	1999 Local Government Act
MBC(s)	Metropolitan borough council(s)
N/A or n/a	Not applicable
NATT	National Association of Teachers of Travellers
NGO(s)	non-governmental organisation(s)
ODPM	Office of the Deputy Prime Minister (May 2002 to date)
OfSTED	Office for Standards in Education
SCF	Save the Children Fund
SEU	Social Exclusion Unit
SSSI	Site of Special Scientific Interest
TLAST	Telephone Legal Advice Service for Travellers
TLRU	Traveller Law Research Unit at Cardiff Law School
UA(s)	Unitary authority(ies)
UE(s)	Unauthorised encampment(s)
UN	United Nations
UNHRC	United Nations Human Rights Committee

DEDICATION

In memory of Eli
In thanks to Sylvia
And to all the other fighters, travelling and settled

ONE

Introduction

Pitfalls of research on costs

This book treads a dangerous line, concerned as it is with costs: the costs borne by the Travelling and non-Travelling communities as a consequence of the former having insufficient and inappropriate accommodation.

The line is a dangerous one for many reasons. Most obviously because it might suggest that social exclusion and human misery are amenable to a simple analysis of costs and benefits. This cannot, of course, be the case, as the following chapters clearly demonstrate.

A less obvious, but equally serious, danger is that which is inherent in all 'quantification' exercises of this nature − that by particularising the cost of everything, little or nothing of value is revealed. This again is a danger which we also hope we have avoided.

This study is based on research carried out between 1999 and 2001, including a survey of all of the local authorities in the United Kingdom. The survey focused on the costs that these authorities had incurred as a consequence of inadequate provision of accommodation for Gypsies and other Travellers. Its importance springs in part from the decision of the 1992-97 government to use 'cost' as a reason for abandoning a long-standing duty on local authorities to provide Gypsy sites. It had argued that expenditure of £5 million per annum (the approximate cost of providing sites) could not be justified. What is extraordinary about this decision is that it was underwritten by no regulatory or financial appraisal: that no attempt was made to ascertain the cost implications of not making any provision.

The idea behind the research study is not original − many commentators both inside and outside Parliament have pointed to the lack of such an appraisal as evidence that the 1994 Criminal Justice and Public Order Act was misconceived. The research results discussed in this book are therefore of great significance. They give both qualitative and quantitative expression to the consequences of abandoning the site provision duty, in part using as an investigative device the disciplines of 'Best Value': an appraisal mechanism introduced by the 1997-2001 government.

To conduct this analysis risks perpetuating the greatest danger of all; namely the maintenance of the costs debate itself. Why is it that so much of the debate is conducted in the language of exchequer expenditure? Why did the figure of a total of £56 million[1] loom so large in the 1992-94 debate? Why is the widespread myth that Gypsies and other Travellers do not pay tax or rent so often repeated? Why does the media constantly dwell on the costs of clearing unauthorised sites and no other contextual issues?

Although the full answer to these questions may lie beyond the remit of this book, the intrinsic danger should form a backdrop to the subsequent analysis – for it is at least arguable that the language of cost in this context is the language of intolerance. It may be that as a society we count the cost of that which we do not value. That by constantly recording the cost of accommodating Travelling People we are articulating a racist and rhetorical question – namely whether we can afford them; that the sum total of Travelling cultures can be expressed in negative financial terms.

Background to the research

As noted, one of the primary motives given for the 1994 legal reforms was financial: that the cost to the public purse of providing sites for Travelling People was unjustifiably high. It is perhaps obvious, but needs stating, that much of the cost arising from unlawful stopping is directly related to the availability and appropriateness of *lawful* stopping places. Research commissioned by the Department of the Environment, Transport and the Regions (DETR)[2] – which, with the Home Office, had key responsibility for matters relating to unlawful stopping or 'unauthorised encampments' – acknowledges this connection, in outlining many possible reasons for unauthorised 'camping':

> Authorised sites may be full, with waiting lists; they may be undesirable, because of, for example, the state of their amenities or relationship breakdown with other occupiers of the site; or there may be no authorised sites in an area. (Cowan et al, 2001, p 5)

Even before the 1994 changes, the issue of unauthorised encampments was clearly viewed as a financial issue by local authorities and others. Earlier government-commissioned research has identified costs as an important factor in how encampments should be approached; over ten years ago one very thorough report stressed that:

> In order to promote political acceptance of formal site provision[3] LAs [local authorities] are recommended to move towards accurate and full accounting of all expenditure with regard to unauthorised gypsy encampments.... Highlighting the direct and indirect costs of non-provision is an excellent way of helping Members to realise that grant-aided site provision is often a far less financially costly means of achieving the goal of an appropriate site policy. However, it is clear that Members do not always wish to face the reality that such figures could offer them.... Few Districts [have] engaged in the practice of fully costing all gypsy-related expenditures, and some explicitly avoided it.... It is clear that many Districts spend several times as much per

annum on such procedures as they would do on running one or more authorised sites for the same gypsies. (Todd and Clark, 1991, p 23)

Independent of the TLRU research reported here, many examples of local authority concern as to costs already exist:[4]

- Milton Keynes Council has reckoned that it spends between £50,000 and £75,000 per year on clearing up unauthorised encampments after they have ended (Milton Keynes Council, 1997). It estimated that in the financial year 1997/98 alone the cost of dealing with unauthorised encampments had been £360,000 (Milton Keynes Council, 1999), and that encampments had discouraged some potential investment and job-creating ventures from setting up in the area.
- The minutes of an Essex County Council meeting (7 June 1999) state that "clearing up after the eviction of large groups of Travellers cost Essex Authorities £45,000 in the last 12 months in respect of public land. No information is available as to the extra cost of clearing up private land."
- Isle of Wight Council minutes (13 April 1999) record that "the costs of managing travellers on the island over the last three years' [1996-99] totalled £22,000".
- Hereford and Worcester County Council minutes (29 September 1995) state that "[i]n resource terms the County Council had to engage in over 40 actions for the possession of land between 1 March 1995 and 25 August 1995. These cases consumed over 472 hours of officer time within the legal department alone." The minutes further record that:

> Comparable amounts of time have been expended by officers of the Directorate of Environmental Services. In addition to staff time there has also been the court costs, the costs of the physical eviction of caravans, measures to deter further occupation, cleansing and the cost of work passed to external legal firms when the need occurs ... the feeling is also growing on the part of County Council officers that eviction action has in too many instances resulted merely in the displacement of the problem from one part of the County to another, some caravans only moving a matter of a few hundred yards.... Furthermore, most of those who are subject to this process of virtually continuous proceedings do not have the prospect of access to local authority sites and are not and will not be eligible for permanent housing. The County Council officers feel that this is not an effective use of resources.

There exists therefore widespread concern, not only about the amount of money and other resources expended on unauthorised encampments, but also as to the wisdom of such expenditure. Paradoxically, while current policy relating to accommodation for Travelling People was originally informed by the costs of site provision, no research had been conducted concerning the costs of non-provision of authorised and appropriate sites.

A pilot study

In order to fill this lacuna, in 1997 the Traveller Law Research Unit (TLRU) at Cardiff Law School undertook a pilot assessment of local authority expenditure resulting from unauthorised encampments of Travelling People. The information gathered included expenditure in terms of officer time, engineering costs – clearing and making sites secure – and the simple legal costs of contested court hearings. Based on a survey response rate of 55%, the assessment indicated that these costs (to unitary authorities, metropolitan and London borough councils, and county councils) might well be in excess of £7 million per annum (see Appendix B for further details).

The final conjectural figure of £7 million did not include money and time spent by planning departments; the police; public landowners and trustees such as the National Trust, railway operators, water authorities, the Forestry Commission and the Ministry of Defence; and private landowners. Nor did it include the costs to the health, security, culture and education of Travelling People and their children, or the attendant future social costs of raising standards within and for these groups. Nor did the study include an estimate of the costs in Scotland or Northern Ireland.

Research into the costs borne by local authorities in relation to unauthorised encampments of Travelling People is an area in which the DETR/DTLR has expressed considerable interest. The department has referred to the TLRU pilot study on several occasions as evidence that 'Best Value' (see further in Chapter Five) may not be supported by simple 'non-toleration policies' in respect of encampments. By way of example, research conducted at Birmingham University, which accompanied and informed the DETR and Home Office guidance *Managing unauthorised camping: A good practice guide*, made reference to the TLRU pilot study as the only research carried out to date in this area (Niner et al, 1998, pp 23-4). The Birmingham research concluded that costs are:

> (a) ... borne by local council tax payers while the offenders are most unlikely to make any contribution to the local tax base; nor, since Gypsies/Travellers often move from one area to another, is it normally perceived as a properly 'local' issue.

> (b) ... the expenditure is incurred in the context of cuts, controls, and caps which restrict council spending on 'desirable' services or provision. One authority argued against having a specific budget for Gypsy/Traveller matters, or quantifying costs too closely since it might draw unwelcome attention from local politicians, or become part of regular budget cutting exercises.

> (c) ... expenditure is seen as wasted in the sense that nothing is solved by the action – at best the authority has shifted the 'problem' (the encampment) across its boundaries. (Niner et al, 1998, p 25)

As a 1999 DETR letter to the TLRU noted, the relevant Minister had "made it clear"[5] that he was keen for local authorities to think "laterally" about the costs of eviction and clearing up, and in particular to consider whether a proportion of these sums "might be more effectively spent on the provision of temporary sites".

Notwithstanding the general concurrence of central and local government that the costs of unauthorised encampments were an important element of policy formulation concerning unauthorised encampments, still no in-depth research had been conducted into this important subject. Accordingly, in 1999 the TLRU gained funding from the Joseph Rowntree Charitable Trust to undertake this more comprehensive review of the issues. (A copy of the questions asked of local authorities in this later and more in-depth study can be seen in Appendix C.)

Unauthorised encampments – definitions and context

Unauthorised encampments (also known as 'unauthorised camping') have been variously described as a "group of caravans or vehicles camped on land without consent to do so" (DETR/Home Office, 1998, p 7); and also as "a scourge on decent people who find their decent lives interrupted and intruded upon" (Duncan, 1999). The first, formal and objective definition does not require that the land concerned is owned by people other than those creating the encampment. (Unauthorised encampments also involve people residing on land that is in their ownership, but who have not been granted permission under planning legislation to use their land for this purpose. The issue of Travelling People and the planning system is discussed further in Chapters Two and Four.) The latter 'definition' indicates the intensity of reaction that such encampments not infrequently occasion.

The UK government estimates that at "any one time there are likely to be around 5,000 Gypsy or Traveller caravans on unauthorised encampments in England" (DETR/Home Office, 1998, p 7). It does not mention any other groups of people in relation to unauthorised encampments in its publications on the subject (nor does it estimate how many caravans there might be in other parts of the UK). This implies that when speaking of people 'creating' and residing on unauthorised encampments, only 'Travelling People' (a definition of this term follows) are the subjects[6].

Unauthorised encampments of Travelling People and their homes and vehicles can take many different forms and affect a large proportion of local government bodies, according to government-commissioned research (Cowan et al, 2001, p 12). Of 243 respondent authorities in England in 2000/01, 92% had Gypsy and Traveller groups camping in unauthorised locations within their area in the previous 12 months; only five appeared to have had none at all in the previous five years. The survey uncovered a wide variation, not only in terms of the numbers of unauthorised sites used by Gypsies and Travellers, but also the number of separate incidents of unauthorised camping. ('Separate incidents' refers to different groups of people using a particular site, as well as the same group moving around different locations within local authority boundaries.) The 2001 research found that unauthorised camping is a prevalent phenomenon, but that for the most part it is relatively small in scale, both in number of locations and separate incidents. Encampment sizes vary; but those involving a dozen caravans or less are much more common than those of 20 or more.

There may, from time to time, be people other than Travelling People stopping on land without express permission. This can include picnickers, drivers taking rest, vacationing caravanners stopping for vehicle repairs or other reasons, and those engaged in recreational pursuits (such as horse riders and off-road cyclists) stopping for food or rest. It is likely that these uses of land are seen as legitimate temporary uses, and are rarely seen as problematic by British society generally. Whatever the reason, there appears to be no question that such uses are not generally assumed to fall within the meaning of 'unauthorised encampments'.

For example, the response of the Countryside Commission to the 1992 consultation paper on reform of the 1968 Caravan Sites Act (see further in Chapter Two) stated that it did not wish "to see overnight camping with tents by walkers, cyclists and other recreational users of the countryside, usually in wild and remote places, become a criminal offence.... Perhaps you could make it clearer that the Government's intentions relate to the occupation of land by caravans rather than tents". The Commission's response was not alone in expressing this type of concern. As another example, the Ramblers' Association warned that it would "scrutinise carefully any forthcoming legislation and shall make representations against it if it appears to us that it could lead to the criminalisation of trespass by walkers, or if it could otherwise unreasonably impinge upon people's peaceful enjoyment of the countryside".

The TLRU study also adopts the 'nomadism-focused' approach in its examination of unauthorised encampments and associated costs. This is not to imply agreement that only Travelling People should fall within strict legislation and regulation of temporary land use, but for the practical reason that the focus here is on the relationship between Travelling People and those who control land use, in the context of 'costs', both human and financial.

The nature of unauthorised encampments

The nature of unauthorised encampments was also explored during the research carried out by Birmingham University (Niner et al, 1998), which informed the DETR and Home Office guidance on *Managing unauthorised camping*; from which some 'significant points' emerged.

The research found that encampments are more of an issue in some areas than others because of the number and scale experienced. This is often related to employment opportunities for Travelling People, traditional routes taken and socio-economic events such as festivals and horse fairs; a considerable proportion of travelling could therefore be predicted. Different Travelling groups have different characteristics and patterns of behaviour, and appear to attract different levels of 'acceptability' from settled people.

Sites subject to encampment are highly variable, and include car parks, derelict land, public recreation areas and industrial estates in urban areas; highway verges and 'droves' or 'green lanes' in rural areas. Naturally, it is those sites that directly affect settled people that attain the highest profile, sometimes generating a large number of complaints and even direct action (or the threat of it). Site 'protection', which aims to deter entrance onto land by means of ditching, earth bunding, gating or other measures, can reduce encampments, but it is then inevitable that Travelling People will move to another unauthorised site (DETR/Home Office, 1998, pp 9-10).

The *Good practice guide* also notes that because Travelling People:

> ... by definition, move on, the number of separate encampments in any year is likely to be significant (number unknown). Paradoxically, the faster Gypsies and Travellers move on (or are moved on) the more encampments result. Eviction action may have the effect of shifting the 'problem' of an encampment elsewhere, not necessarily to a more appropriate site, or even to one in a different local authority area. (p 9)

Use of the term 'unauthorised' does not imply that an unauthorised encampment is in itself illegal, in the sense of being contrary to the criminal code (although it may be, for example by obstructing the highway or by being contrary to section 61, 1994 Criminal Justice and Public Order Act). 'Unauthorised' does not even imply that an encampment is unlawful by contravening civil law (although it will often constitute a trespass). It is not what has been done, but what has not been done, that makes an encampment 'unauthorised'. It may be in no way antisocial, may be entirely beneficial and may indeed be on land owned by the Gypsy or Traveller. Nevertheless, it is 'unauthorised' because it lacks administrative approval, most obviously the necessary land use planning approval.

Many encampments are 'tolerated' in the sense that they are not subject to concerted enforcement action, but many are not. Frequently, the determining factor between toleration and eviction will not be the behaviour of the Travelling People or the impact on the land or local community of their encampment, but the administrative policies of the local authority (or indeed lack of such policies). Such policies may be informed by the principles of Best Value; however, as this study discloses, they will generally not be so informed.

Unlawful behaviour does not therefore exist in a vacuum. It is too simplistic to speak of Travelling People creating unauthorised encampments. 'Unauthorised encampments' are a socio-legal construct.

> [S]ocial groups create deviance by making the rules whose infraction constitutes deviance, and by applying those rules to particular people and labelling them as outsiders.... Differences in the ability to make rules and apply them to other people are essentially power differentials (either legal or extralegal). Those groups whose social position gives them weapons and power are best able to enforce their rules. (Becker, 1963, p 9 and pp 17-18)

Travelling is generally seen as legitimate[7] and is largely unproblematic. However, to travel as a way of life presupposes some ability to stop occasionally, and it is the case that stopping often engages the law. The law is drafted, implemented and enforced by a society within which a 'settled' way of life is the favoured option of the majority. The mores of this majority have been entrenched in various ways and given explicit endorsement in government guidance. A Department of the Environment (DoE) Circular (DoE and Welsh Office, 1994a), for instance, directs that local authorities should use their powers "to afford a higher level of protection to private owners of land" (p 3).

Who unauthorised encampments concern

The *Good practice guide* summarises local authority involvement with the issue of unauthorised encampments as follows:

> Local authorities become involved as owners of land subject to encampment or in support of other landowners, as the recipients of complaints from the public, and as service providers to citizens including Gypsies and Travellers. Local authorities also have the power – between 1970 and 1994, the duty – to provide and manage Gypsy sites and, as local planning authorities, to consider applications for site development from Gypsies and Travellers themselves. (DETR/Home Office, 1998, p 7)

In addition to the other parties implicitly identified in that statement – private landowners (including farmers and business interests), Travelling People, non-Travelling People resident in communities near unauthorised encampments – the police, local and national politicians, national and local media, lawyers, planners, public service providers and Gypsy and Traveller organisations will also at times be concerned with or by the issue of unauthorised encampments.

Estimates vary widely as to the number of Travelling People in the UK. As will be discussed in the next chapter, official counts are almost certainly significant underestimates. However, it is likely that Travelling People number no more than 300,000; that is to say, less than half of one percent of the UK population. Notwithstanding that this represents such a small proportion, unauthorised encampments are an issue that appears to affect a large number and range of people. This is reflected not least by annual discussions of unauthorised encampments in Parliament[8] and the large number of encampment-related articles appearing regularly in local and national newspapers (Morris, 2000).

Travelling People

For the purposes of this publication, the term 'Travelling People' is employed to embrace all those who are, have been or will be associated with a potentially nomadic way of life. This includes the 'minority ethnic groups' recognised as such under the 1976 Race Relations Act (as amended, 2000) and known as

Romany Gypsies (whether English, Scottish or Welsh) and Irish Travellers; whether mobile, of limited mobility or not living a constantly mobile way of life but settled in housing or in caravans on public or private sites[9]. It also includes so-called 'new' Travellers, some of whom are second, third or fourth generation Travellers, and some of whom have Gypsy or other Traveller antecedents (Kenrick and Clark, 1999; Morris and Clements, 1999).

As there are significant cultural and other differences between these 'groups', the term 'Travelling People' should not be taken to imply a single and culturally homogeneous community. Nonetheless, the issues that affect those people who fall within the term as used here, including accommodation, security of tenure, education and costs, are sufficiently similar to group them together for this purpose.

In 1994 the Children's Society carried out research as to why the newest Travelling People, first generation Travellers, had adopted a nomadic way of life (Davis et al, 1994). Some may have taken to the road because of a shortage of affordable housing or for personal, 'push' rather than 'pull', reasons. Only one third of those involved in the study had made a conscious and deliberate choice to travel. "The image of the typical traveller as a middle class, educated person who chooses to travel as an alternative to other viable options was therefore not borne out by the study" (Davis et al, 1994, p 6).

There are groups of people who may, for other purposes, also be encompassed by the phrase 'Travelling People'. However, it is self-evident that research on unauthorised encampments must focus mainly on those people who are associated with such encampments. For this reason, fairground and circus families are not usually implied by the term as, aside from occasional planning matters, these communities are not generally identified by settled society as causing encampment 'problems'.

Notes

[1] The estimated cumulative cost of providing Gypsy sites between 1980 and 1992.

[2] Renamed Department of Transport, Local Government and the Regions (DTLR) in May 2001; from May 2002 the functions are part of the Office of the Deputy Prime Minister (ODPM).

[3] This report was written at a time when local authorities had a duty to provide sites for Gypsies. This period is dealt with in greater detail in Chapter Two.

[4] More examples of costs and attitudes relating to unauthorised encampments can be found in Appendix A.

[5] Speech to the Inaugural Annual General Meeting of the National Association of Gypsy and Traveller Officers (NAGTO), Coventry, October 1998.

[6] Although there are naturally periodic exceptions to every general rule. One local authority respondent to the TLRU research noted that most costs in the period were incurred in respect of 'squatters' (who were not Travelling People) evicted from housing in the area.

[7] As is avowed by the current government, or at least the DTLR/ODPM.

[8] In 1999 alone, debates took place or questions were raised in the House of Commons about 'Travellers' on 18 March, 10 May, 19 July and 1 November.

[9] In this work, the words 'Gypsy(ies)', 'Traveller(s)' and 'Travelling People' are capitalised to reflect that the words are proper nouns, in the same vein as 'Jewish' and 'Irish', except where they are not so capitalised and/or are misspelled in the original.

TWO

Past and present law

Travelling People within the UK have never enjoyed a Golden Age. Although legal restrictions on the Travelling way of life have multiplied over the last hundred years, it is probable that prior legal and extra-legal restrictions were every bit as oppressive.

The enclosure of common land undoubtedly affected Travelling People no less than other landless people, as did the more recent decline in demand for manual labour due to farm mechanisation. Social change and legal regulation have inevitably marched together. Their combined impact has been to curtail the possibility of (and possibilities for) a nomadic way of life. Differences exist among legal commentators as to which statutes have proved to be the most oppressive in terms of tightening the restrictions faced by Travelling People. In reality, the screw has been turning steadily, at least since Gypsies first came to the UK five or six hundred years ago (Mayall, 1995).

As will be discussed, Mr Justice Sedley (now Lord Justice Sedley) considered the regulatory impact of the 1960 Caravan Sites and Control of Development Act to be a crucial marker, as other commentators to whom he referred had highlighted provisions within that Act restricting access to remaining common land. Yet others have emphasised the impact of the 1947 Town and Country Planning Act or the restrictions on highway camping contained in the 1959 Highways Act.

As ever, however, the story is more complex. Public regulation of the commons (including the prohibition of camping) dates back to at least the Commons Acts of the late 1800s and early 1900s, and the 1925 Law of Property Act. The control of development substantially predates the 1947 Act and highway use has always been the subject of robust policing.

In retrospect, it is possible to subdivide post-World War Two legislative history, as it has impacted on Travelling People, into three distinct phases. The first 25 years (until 1969) was a period that witnessed a vast growth in regulations, which (albeit incrementally) created enormous problems for Travelling People. In response to these problems, legislation was enacted that sought to remedy some of the difficulties. This, the second phase, can be characterised as the consensus years. The final (and present) phase has seen the rise of a new intolerance that views Gypsies and other Travellers as being the 'problem', rather than the problem being the social regulatory system that has effectively outlawed their way of life.

Incrementalism: 1944 to 1969

Although in many ways the incremental years had the most negative impact on the Travelling tradition, what marks them out (from previous periods) was the fact that this was not deliberate. The raison d'etre for each landmark statute, be it the 1947 Town and Country Planning Act, the 1959 Highways Act or the 1960 Caravan Sites and Control of Development Act, was *not* to curtail the Travelling way of life; the severe restrictions created by these Acts were in large measure unintended consequences.

Liégeois (1987, p 111) has referred to this situation as "an accumulation of handicaps ... the combined effects of [which] transform nomadism into vagrancy". Planning controls are entirely reasonable in an overcrowded island; highway restrictions are necessary, given that the UK has the most congested roads in Europe; environmental controls are essential in modern Western European states and cannot be properly enforced without a system of licensing; and so on. The overall impact of these, however, may not always be so rational.

It was this 'incrementalism' that was at the heart of the first Gypsy case to be heard by the European Court of Human Rights, *Buckley v UK* (1996) 25 September, 23 EHRR 101. Judge Pettiti identified and described the phenomenon in his dissenting opinion:

> The Strasbourg institutions' difficulty in identifying this type of problem is that the deliberate superimposition and accumulation of administrative rules (each of which would be acceptable taken singly) result, firstly, in its being totally impossible for a Gypsy family to make suitable arrangements for its accommodation, social life and the integration of its children at school, and secondly, in different government departments combining measures relating to town planning, nature conservation, the viability of access roads, planning permission requirements, road safety and public health that, in the instant case, mean the Buckley family are caught in a "vicious circle".

The effect of 25 years of regulatory restrictions on Travelling and the wholesale loss of traditional stopping places have been well documented (Adams et al, 1975). It was to resolve these largely unintended consequences that specific legislation, in the guise of the 1968 Caravan Sites Act, was enacted.

Consensus years: public site provision 1970 to 1992

Before 1960, Travelling People had significantly less trouble in finding sites for their caravans. However, the 1960 Caravan Sites and Control of Development Act introduced special controls to prevent unauthorised caravan sites, and required that sites should obtain planning permission along with a special site license. This Act was intended to control leisure caravans or mobile homes and to prevent the growth of unsightly caravan sites in rural areas. Unfortunately, it took no account of the needs of Travelling People. Even when they could find sympathetic farmers willing to let them leave their caravans on fields, that remained illegal without planning permission, except for a very short stay.

As a result of these difficulties, Eric Lubbock MP (now Lord Avebury) introduced a Private Member's Bill, which subsequently became the 1968 Caravan Sites Act (CSA) and came into force in 1970. The Act placed a duty on local authorities to provide sites for Gypsies "residing in or resorting to" their area. Additionally, it enabled authorities that had provided 'sufficient' sites for such Gypsies to attain 'designation' status, which brought with it enhanced powers to evict. Designation was widely criticised as effectively creating a system of 'apartheid' in the areas to which it applied. Indeed, in 1997 the government in Northern Ireland repealed designation provisions within its law, explicitly accepting that they were discriminatory[1].

In its early years the CSA had only a limited impact as many local authorities failed to develop any Gypsy sites, even with the incentive of 'designation' powers. Accordingly the government commissioned an inquiry into the operation of the Act, which was carried out by John Cripps and published in 1976. Among its many conclusions and recommendations, the Cripps Report stated that:

> It must surely be possible ... for the majority to come to terms with a minority, albeit non-conforming, who number fewer than 50,000, if gypsies now living in houses are excluded. Certainly it is in the interest of the majority to do this rather than to ... incur the avoidable cost of evictions, fencing and trenching, and makeshift arrangements to the tune of hundred of thousands of pounds annually.... Time costs money, and the amount of time now being spent by government officials, by members and officers of local government, by the courts and members of the police and probation services, and by individuals in numerous capacities is out of all relation to the size of the problem. (Cripps, 1976, p 1)

Although, following the Cripps Report, the 1980 Local Government Act introduced a further incentive for Gypsy site provision in the form of 100% exchequer grants to cover the costs, many local authorities still did not create sufficient – or, in some cases, any – sites. This failure can be attributed to a number of factors, perhaps most crucially a dearth of political will at both local and national levels. This includes the failure of the Secretary of State to use available powers of direction under section 9 of the CSA to compel authorities to meet their duty. These powers were employed only five times, and on each occasion the Secretary of State was forced to use them following decisions of judicial review.

Hawes and Perez have identified eight weaknesses in the CSA that they suggest should not be replicated in future legislation: failure to recognise differing pressures in different constituencies and circumstances; failure to differentiate between the various needs of different Travelling People; conflict and lack of cohesion and leadership created by splitting provisionary and management roles between county and district councils; spending on sites having to compete against more popular priorities for annual spending estimates, as the grant counted against overall capital allocation; lack of demographic data about current and future populations and needs of Travelling People; lack of relationship between the provisionary duty and the need to ensure provision of other services; lack of recognition of disadvantage, ethnicity and related social policy issues within the provision framework; and the designation policy being:

> [A] device alien to the main thrust of the Act, representing a prejudicial and inherently anti-Traveller mechanism striking at the heart of any concept of respect and recognition of the validity of Gypsy culture. It was seen by authorities as a 'carrot' or prize for doing the minimum it was possible to get away with, and the minister's failure to use his directional powers until quite late in the process reinforced the understanding. (1996, p 49-50)

The CSA was, however, by no means a complete failure. The philosophy underlying its reform in 1994 (if such existed) was probably the concept of replacing public with private provision: the private sector (primarily Gypsies and other Travellers themselves) providing the sites that the public sector had failed to provide. This was based on the mistaken premise that public provision had failed, whereas it had in fact achieved a great deal in terms of sheer numbers of pitches. Despite the apparent quadrupling of Gypsy caravan numbers in the intervening period (1965 to 1994), the unauthorised encampment figure had been reduced from 80 to 30 percent (Clements and Smith, 1997, p 64).

Modern intolerance: 1992 to the present

Reform of the 1968 Caravan Sites Act

In announcing the review of the CSA in 1992, Housing and Planning Minister Sir George Young stated that "[the Act] has become an open-ended commitment to provide sites, which inevitably leads to a drain on the taxpayer's money and undermines gypsies' responsibilities to provide for themselves" (*The Independent*, 19 August 1992)[2]. Although the review coincided with concerns over 'raves' and other large-scale outdoor events raising potential public order problems, the Minister stressed that the measures were "not designed to tackle the public order issues which arise when huge numbers of New Age Travellers congregate unexpectedly".

In August 1992 the government issued a consultation paper on the reform of the CSA. There were 993 officially recognised responses to this paper out of approximately 1,400. (The remainder were mostly "from Gypsies who failed for various reasons to structure their responses in the required manner"; Campbell, 1995, p 28.) This is a particularly substantial response to a paper on what was, in the context of government business generally, a relatively small and specialised matter. However, it appears that there was little governmental reaction to the majority of responses received. (The text of the 1992 consultation paper itself, and extracts from selected responses to it by a variety of individuals and organisations, are in Appendix D.)

A Department of the Environment (DoE) analysis of some responses to the paper from 'Gypsies, New Age Travellers and Gypsy Organisations' (unpublished, 25 November 1992) found that, out of 34 responses, one accepted the proposals with reservations, but the remainder counselled against them. The analysis noted that the "overwhelming view from the gypsies' side of the fence is that the proposals represent an attack on basic human rights, and are designed to stop them travelling for good ... the phrase 'ethnic cleansing' was used by several respondents".

Seventeen of these 34 responses pointed out that some local authorities had not met their duty under the CSA. Several respondents requested that, rather than remove the duty to provide sites, authorities that had not provided sufficient accommodation should be compelled to do so following direction by the Secretary of State. Another respondent expressed the view that local authorities that had not complied with the duty were being rewarded for unlawful behaviour.

According to the DoE analysis, almost one third of these respondents expressed deep concern at a proposal in the paper to seize caravans, citing the possible social problems that could result, including children being taken into care or families being forced into bed and breakfast accommodation. One such response drew comparisons between the cost of housing a family in such accommodation and that of providing a lawful place to park; several others believed the proposal would lead to an increase in homelessness.

An analysis of local authority responses to the 1992 consultation paper conducted by Cecily Taylor for the Advisory Council for the Education of Romany and other Travellers (ACERT) found the tone of the responses to be as shown in Table 2.1.

These results appear to indicate that most authorities did not support, or were sceptical of, the efficacy of the proposals. They also suggest that, while

Table 2.1: Analysis of local authority responses to the 1992 consultation paper on reform of the 1968 Caravan Sites Act

	County councils	London boroughs and metropolitan authorities	District councils
The proposals do not provide workable solutions	43/46: 93%	36/39: 92%	170/239: 71%
Retain the statutory duty to provide sites	26/46: 56%	22/39: 56%	115(+9*)/239: 48(51*)%
Retain 100% funding	34(+2*)/46: 73(78*)%	24(+2*)/39: 61(66*)%	127(+5*)/239 53(55*)%
Distinguish between Gypsies and New Travellers	31/46: 67%	8/39: 20%	91/239: 38%

* By implication.

many authorities wished to continue to play a role in enabling sites for Gypsies, they would need more encouragement to take the same steps for those they perceived not to be 'traditional' Travelling People.

Concerns as to costs

A number of the responses to the DoE consultation paper[3] expressed concern about the costs of the proposals, were they to be effected.

The Save the Children Fund (SCF) stated that the "implication that the Travelling population is unduly subsidised at public expense, and that the proposed measures will reduce public subsidy to Travellers is both unhelpful and misleading". SCF pointed out that the occupants of local authority caravan sites, like local authority tenants (site occupants are mere licensees), pay rent and other charges, sometimes at a higher rate than housed people. As an example, SCF noted that while council rents had risen by 44% since 1990, Gypsies in Hertfordshire had experienced rent increases more in the range of 60 to 63 percent. SCF believed that the decision to remove the exchequer grant would "simply shift the financial responsibility to local authorities. The public expenditure costs of many of the proposals ... go unmentioned. These would be enormous and would fall on the police, the judicial system, the prison system and local authorities".

The Police Federation of England and Wales was also concerned about the possible costs to their services, responding that any reduction in site provision would "result in increasing numbers of travellers roaming from county to county and exacerbating the problem, thereby placing a further drain upon police resources brought about by increased workloads". The County Landowners Association also thought that the police already lacked resources, fearing that if site and service provision issues were not resolved "the problem of mass trespass of land can and will get worse. The repeal of the Caravan Sites Act will not address those problems and will in some ways exacerbate the problems of a distinct and separate section of the community".

Wiltshire County Council was critical of the paper's failure to assess the costs or savings potential of alternative policies:

> No information is provided on the percentage of this expenditure [£56 million] which has been incurred by local authorities in obtaining and retaining designation, nor the cost of saving this has brought to those authorities as a result of not having to take action to move illegal encampments let alone the problems for the public, members and officers that these encampments cause. The paper is equally silent on the undoubted costs that all local authorities will be faced with in enforcing the new powers including the costs of the homeless.

The Religious Society of Friends (Quaker Social Responsibility and Education) complained that: "It is offensive to call the provision of sites a 'relentless drain on taxpayers' funds'. Would the same phrase be used to describe the provision of much more costly local authority housing or mortgage relief?" The Society referred to the government's own research as showing that local authorities that fail to provide sites often spend much more on eviction costs than a proper site would cost to set up (Todd and Clark, 1991).

The London Housing Aid Centre (SHAC) stated that £56 million was not a great deal of money to spend over a 14-year period on a countrywide policy. The National Gypsy Council calculated that the average cost per pitch of constructing a site was considerably less than the construction costs of council housing. The National Farmers Union was concerned that few new authorised sites would be established if statutory duties were repealed, leading to an increase in the number of encampments; asserting that "there would be the risk of significant resources being expended on merely moving the illegal encampments from one area to another".

The Law Centres Federation was concerned that the burden on "already over-stretched Housing Authorities" would be increased by Travelling People having little alternative other than to make applications. "This will in turn lead to greater costs for those Housing Authorities, and the placing of the families in unsuitable and expensive temporary accommodation". Kent County Council shared the concern of its district councils that land allocated for housing "has a much higher value than the type of land in rural areas normally used for Gypsy caravan sites. Whilst Gypsy families might occupy more land, the overall costs within a caravan site are less than for housing".

The Gypsy Council for Education, Culture, Welfare and Civil Rights believed that the figure of £56 million would "pale into insignificance given the costs of evictions", within which would be included bed and breakfast accommodation, prisons, children's homes, local authority housing, the costs of storing caravans and other possessions, court proceedings, police and council manpower, shattered lives, and "ditching and banking". The Association of Local Authorities also had concerns in relation to cost-effectiveness, stating that in London, with over 40,000 households at that time already in temporary accommodation, "there is no realistic alternative and compared to the cost of hotels the use of sites is the best solution … [on a site] there are the twin benefits of enabling households to remain together and enabling children to gain education and other services".

Canterbury City Council expressed the view that, if permanent housing were to be provided for each family on local authority sites, the increase in capital provision required would be "phenomenal". It added that a great deal of the Council's time and money was spent "moving groups of gypsies round and round the district and the resultant treks to the Magistrates Court which happen once or twice a week are both time-consuming and expensive" (£24,138 had recently been spent on 38 cases, £6,400 of which was recouped from private landowners after action taken on their behalf and the remainder spent on evictions from council land).

Cardiff Gypsy Sites Group feared that the proposals would prevent professionals in statutory agencies providing services related to education, health, social services and welfare benefits, and specialist service providers such as Gypsy Liaison Officers, "from offering constructive help, advice, emergency support or treatment. The resultant increase in evictions will deprive Gypsy Travellers and their children of opportunities for preventative health screening by dentists, doctors, midwives or health visitors".

As one of the many individuals who responded to the consultation paper, Lord Lucas of Crudwell wrote to say that his principal concern was financial in nature and that he did not believe that "in these straightened times any measure could be considered without an assessment being made of its financial impact ... it was you who introduced [£56 million] into the argument, presumably as an indication of 'savings'. So will you supply me with some figures, or must I put down a question?"

These substantial quotations are in fact a tiny (although, TLRU having read every response, representative) proportion of the overall response to the consultation paper. That the costs of unauthorised encampments are a common concern among a wide range of bodies and persons and have been for some time is markedly clear. Nonetheless, government policy and resultant legislation has seemingly been formulated without reference to this disquiet.

The Criminal Justice and Public Order Bill

Questions concerning the human, social and financial impact of the measures were again raised in 1994, when most of the measures proposed in 1992 were put before Parliament in the Criminal Justice and Public Order Bill. One of the few proposals dropped in the light of consultation responses was that local authorities should have the power to seize caravans as an alternative to imprisonment for non-payment of fines. The 100% exchequer grants for the capital costs of site provision were indeed abolished, as had been announced in the DoE letter of 18 August 1992, which accompanied the release of the consultation paper[4].

During Parliamentary debates, some believed that the £56 million expended on sites between 1970 and 1992 was derisory. In the Standing Committee B 15th sitting on the Bill, Jean Corston MP raised both the quantity of opposition to the legal changes and the comparative financial implications:

> [A] city council told the Department of the Environment that it spent £71,000 in 1990 on evictions from illegal transit camps. The Police Superintendents Association of England and Wales said that the resource implications must be recognised. The Magistrates Association does not wish the duty to be repealed unless adequate alternative provision – embodied in legislation – is made....
>
> There is also a cost in human terms. There is the continuing mess, nuisance and disruption to residents and businesses, and there is the misery, insecurity and ill effects on health and livelihoods for the families kept constantly on the move. It has been a constant problem in my constituency and throughout Avon. Under such circumstances, what hope is there of children attending

school? (House of Commons Standing Committee B, 10 February 1994, cols 710–11)

More in-depth concerns were expressed by David Rendel MP (Newbury) during a Commons debate months later:

[I]f we assume for a moment that the Government want to see an increase in sites, I think they are right, for the following reasons. First, there is all the human cost incurred in leaving a large number of the gipsy population on unauthorised sites. There is a human cost incurred by moving on the gipsies from site to site every few days....

Even if the Government are not prepared to recognise the human cost, surely they should recognise the financial cost involved.... We must also consider the cost to society as a whole. Can we really believe that it is right that the upbringing of children should be disrupted?... If there is a reduction in the increase in the number of authorised sites, the social and other costs to which I have just referred must greatly outweigh a reduction in the cost of the small number of extra sites set up by the gipsies. (House of Commons Weekly Hansard, 10 October 1994, cols 362–3)

Members of the House of Lords were no less forthcoming as to their concerns about the various cost implications. Lord Irvine of Lairg (in 2002, the sitting Lord Chancellor) asserted that:

[T]o make a man a criminal because he fails to move his family and himself when he has nowhere to which he may lawfully go will devalue the criminal law. A person in that position is more in need of assistance than prosecution. It will not enhance respect for the criminal law to treat such practical problems as the occasion of a criminal offence. Secondly, to force a man to move himself and his family when he has nowhere to which he may lawfully go will mean merely that he must camp unlawfully somewhere else. Far from the law helping to solve any problem of unauthorised camping, it will merely transfer it to another location at considerable public expense ... and in defiance of common humanity. (House of Lords Weekly Hansard, 11 July to 15 July 1994, cols 1516–17)

Some non-Parliamentary respondents to the 1992 paper also continued to lobby their concerns during the passage of the Bill through Parliament. However, despite expressions of concern from many quarters, the Criminal Justice and Public Order Bill was little amended and received Royal Assent on 3 November 1994.

From Bill to Act: 1994 to 2002

Taken as a whole, there are familiar tones in this construction of the problem that can be seen in relation to other minority groups: the question of numbers (increasing at an unacceptable pace); the refusal to acknowledge differences in culture; the presence of a 'few who spoil it for the rest' (and for whom the rest must pay); the denial of needs that do not conform to established norms (or the denial of different delivery to meet the same needs); the cost of special provision to the exchequer and the 'taxpaying public' (to which, it is assumed, the group in question do not belong); and the 'privileges' accorded to a group that the majority of the population are denied (Lloyd, 1993, p 82).

Gypsy sites continued to be built for a few years after the 1992 consultation paper was issued. Some building works were already in the pipeline before that time and, therefore, the costs of site provision continued to rise. In a DoE press release issued on 3 November 1994, shortly before the Criminal Justice and Public Order Act (CJPOA) came into force, it was said that a total of £87 million had been spent since 1978 on grant aid for site provision.

It was to be expected that the efficacy of the 1994 Act would be a matter for ongoing review by both government departments and non-governmental organisations (NGOs). For instance, an Association of District Councils (ADC, now Local Government Association) announced the findings of its own survey, revealing that "89 per cent of the authorities which replied consider the present regime to be 'poor' or 'unworkable'". Councillor Brian White, then Chair of the ADC Planning Committee, was quoted as saying that the "present situation with travellers being continually moved on from one illegal site to another is highly unsatisfactory. Action must be taken by the Government to address this situation" (press release of 24 April 1996).

The first major research carried out by central government into the use of police powers under the 1994 Act was commissioned by the Home Office (Bucke and James, 1998). The Home Office researchers found the CJPOA provisions "to have been applied to both New Age Travellers and gypsies" (p vii), but also noted that the use of eviction powers varied in relation to different groups of Travelling People and by different police forces.

> In at least two forces visited officers stated that they simply did not use the trespass provisions against gypsies since it was felt that this would be inappropriate. Other forces had used the provisions on numerous occasions to remove gypsies from various sites. However, in at least one force this use of the provisions had been replaced by a new policy that reduced their use to 'extreme cases' involving large disruptive groups and property damage on a large scale. (Bucke and James, 1998, p 7)

The problematic and costly nature of some CJPOA provisions relating to unauthorised encampments, for all parties concerned, was also highlighted in the Home Office research. In one case police had used their powers to seize vehicles. This involved a group of Gypsies with around 30 vehicles, camped on a school playing field, who had not heard of the 1994 Act and were convinced that the police did not have the right to remove them. The superintendent in charge contacted the local authority in order to use its vehicle pounds and to request, if need be, housing for people whose vehicles were seized. A large number of officers were present – extra support having been called for – and they began removing vehicles. Perhaps unsurprisingly, some whose vehicles (including their homes) were seized reacted angrily and resisted, leading to a number of arrests for assault. Further conflict took place at the vehicle pound, resulting in two people taking their homes back and subsequently being prosecuted and fined for theft, as impounded vehicles are legally in police possession (Bucke and James, 1998, p 13).

The research stressed that one resultant cost of eviction was frustration, both for police and landowners. Following eviction, it was common for police to urge landowners to protect land from further unauthorised access; officers sometimes stated that they would not assist in repossession of land in future unless such work was carried out. It was clear that, paradoxically, these frustrations could lead to policies and practices that created yet more encampments and greater frustration. "I have chased one group now for over a year and I have served eight lots of notices on them, from one bit of land to another bit of land, to another bit of land to another bit of land. So you just chase them around" (Bucke and James, 1998, p 15).

This reflects one of the concerns expressed by many respondents to the 1992 paper, that the legal changes would result in yet more encampments. This fear proved to be well founded, according to research undertaken by the Children's Society, which found that evictions on smaller sites tended to result in people moving to a smaller number of larger sites. Anxiety among local residents tends to intensify as the size of a site increases, and eviction is then more likely. The pattern that emerged from the Society's research was that of Travelling People becoming *more* nomadic, mainly as a result of eviction. The 1994 Act then appeared to have "increased the scale and frequency of movement, with the same people moving around a decreasing number of sites. As more sites are blocked or trenched off the search for new sites becomes more desperate with the increased likelihood of more private land being occupied by travellers" (Davis, 1997, p 128).

Since 1994, comments have continued to be made periodically in Parliamentary debates as to the costs and concerns arising from unauthorised encampments. Mr John Carlisle MP (Luton North) said in 1996 that Gypsies and Travellers cost local authorities and individuals "an enormous amount in terms of legal fees, which run to several hundreds of thousands of pounds, if not more, throughout the country.... The estimate of cost to the Luton council tax payer last year was £60,000. I think that was an underestimate of what we had to pay to move the gipsies on, and in getting rid of them altogether" (House of Commons Weekly Hansard, No 1726, cols 226-7) .

The UK governments in power since 1994 (to the present) have continued to assert, both domestically and at European and international levels, that policy and law relating to unauthorised encampments in the UK is useful and fair.

However, evidence exists to suggest that the effect of these laws and policies may not always be of this nature.

At United Nations Human Rights Committee (UNHRC) hearings in July 1995, the UK delegation claimed that those sections of the 1994 CJPOA relating to Gypsies and Travellers were designed specifically to deal only with a "troublesome minority" (Liberty, 1995, p 5). However, the organisation Friends, Families and Travellers (FFT) had monitored the impact of the legislation to date and reported that the new powers had been widely used during the first 12 months against people who were peaceful, quiet and law abiding, at sites where vulnerable individuals such as pregnant women and children were living, and to carry out many unjust and unnecessary evictions. It is not clear whether the government's claims to the UNHRC were "disingenuous or simply ill informed" (Liberty, 1995, p 5).

Numbers of unauthorised encampments

Twice annually, on one particular day in January and July, local authorities in England carry out a count of Gypsy caravans on public and private sites, and on unauthorised encampments[5]. The DTLR/ODPM then collates the information gathered and publishes it.

Even government research has been critical of the worth of biannual counts; there have also been various criticisms from official agencies and Gypsy and Traveller representative groups. In particular, there is doubt as to whether the count provides adequate measures of the need for, and provision of, sites, and concern about the accuracy of the data. Information about Travelling People is also needed for other purposes, not only in the housing field but also for the provision of education and health services.

The recommendations arising from one report commissioned by government included: that families and children should be counted rather than caravans; projections should be made of the future population and their needs; those 'counted' should be interviewed as to their needs and desires; 'new' Travellers should not be included (as this might increase demand for sites); and that a national survey might be carried out to obtain information unobtainable from the counts (Green and OPCS, 1991, p 3). None of these recommendations appears yet to have been implemented.

It is clear then that official estimates of the number of caravans in England and Wales should be treated with caution. Not all local authorities participate in the counts, and those that do may not include those Travelling People whom they deem not to be 'Gypsies' (Geary and O'Shea, 1995). Other counts by statutory and voluntary educational bodies (Cardiff University School of Education, 1998) have put the numbers much higher, in some cases at double the official numbers. No differentiation tends to be made between 'tolerated and unauthorised' and 'intolerable and unauthorised' sites. Nor indeed does the number of caravans provide information as to the number of available pitches in public sites (because, for instance, different sites will permit different numbers of vehicles per pitch).

Table 2.2: Official January counts of caravans on unauthorised encampments in England (1997-2001)

Regions	1997	1998	1999	2000	2001
Greater London	55	152	213	251	146
South East	491	340	424	325	443
Eastern	598	722	588	625	998
South West	288	315	333	325	387
East Midlands	188	289	212	379	191
West Midlands	531	387	460	293	207
North West	209	199	151	79	76
Yorkshire and Humberside	214	158	157	210	117
North	17	22	30	25	43
Total	**2,591**	**2,584**	**2,568**	**2,512**	**2,608**

As stated in the previous chapter, it is extremely difficult to estimate the number of Travelling People themselves. Travelling People are not included in the National Census, except insofar as it is open to them to tick the 'Other' category in the list of minority ethnic groups (Morris, 1999). It is equally difficult to estimate how many Travelling People are settled in housing; how long they will remain there; and why they are now housed. What is certain is that none will easily give up their cultural identity and customs. Many will return to life 'on the road' (Thomas and Campbell, 1992).

Despite these cautionary notes, the biannual counts might at least reveal a pattern year on year of numbers of caravans on types of stopping places. Five of the more recently published January counts of unauthorised encampments are shown in Table 2.2.

Additionally, a supplementary note sent out by the then DETR with the 'Gypsy Counts' (in May 2000) commented that in January 2000 the number of local authority Gypsy sites in England was 319 (5,057 pitches). There was a net decrease of 204 pitches during 1999, taking into account 26 pitches gained on seven existing sites and 19 pitches in two new sites. There were 249 pitches lost on 24 existing sites. A naturally increasing Travelling population, and a clear decrease in available public pitches, suggest that the numbers of unauthorised encampments are likely to increase (unless high numbers of Travelling People resort to conventional housing).

In November 2000 Lord Avebury asked the government how many caravan pitches were provided by local authorities and private persons or landlords respectively, and how many caravans there were on unauthorised encampments, as recorded by the January local authority counts since the information was first collected; and whether the government considered that, in the absence of any new measures, unauthorised encampments would become 'necessary'.

The written reply from the Parliamentary Under-Secretary of State at the DETR, Lord Whitty, stated that when information about the number of pitches was first collected, in January 1982, there were 200 sites, containing a total of

Table 2.3: Percentage of Gypsy caravans on land of differing status (1979 and 2000)

Caravans on:	Public sites	Private sites	Unauthorised sites
January 1979 %	36%	14%	50%
January 2000 %	47%	34%	19%

3,113 pitches. As at January 2000, there were 319 sites, containing 5,057 pitches. (Information about sites provided by private persons or landlords is not collected or recorded by the government.)

Lord Whitty also pointed out that the biannual counts do not provide information about numbers of pitches, but about 'Gypsy' caravans. At January 1979, when the count was first introduced, there were 2,988 caravans on local authority sites, 1,194 on private sites and 4,176 on unauthorised sites (a total of 8,358). As of January 2000, there were 6,118 caravans on local authority sites, 4,500 on private sites and 2,516 on unauthorised sites (totalling 13,134). Lord Whitty's letter stated that, expressed as a percentage of the total number of Gypsy caravans, the figures are shown in Table 2.3.

Lord Whitty also stated the government belief that the figures demonstrate the effectiveness of its policy relating to unauthorised encampments:

> The present policy (of encouraging Gypsies to provide sites for themselves through the planning process, giving clear guidance to local authorities on their powers to deal with unauthorised camping and encouraging local authorities to keep existing local authority sites open) is clearly having an effect in reducing unauthorised camping. (DETR, 2000a)

The assertion is that, because there now seem to be fewer unauthorised encampments as a percentage of caravans overall, the policy of leaving site provision to 'private developers', including (or perhaps only) Travelling People themselves, has proven effective in reducing unauthorised encampments. This, however, is questionable logic, based as it is on snapshot figures on two out of 365 days each year. Even if official counts of unauthorised encampments were accurate and unauthorised encampments were indeed decreasing as a percentage of stopping places, this does not mean that there are now fewer unauthorised encampments overall each year than formerly.

An example of how counts on two days each year cannot provide a picture of the actual scale of unauthorised encampments can be found in South Gloucestershire. The Avon Travellers Support Group notes that, in addition to the biannual Gypsy caravan counts, South Gloucestershire Council maintains a daily running total of unauthorised encampments. The DETR figures stated that there were 83 unauthorised encampments in the South Gloucestershire area between 21 July 1999 and 16 July 2000. The authority counted 826 during the period, and the Support Group suggests that this too is an underestimate, as five sites known by the Group to have experienced unauthorised encampments in the period were not officially recorded (Avon Travellers Support Group correspondence to the TLRU, January 2000).

That the counts cannot be relied on to support the assertion that current policy results in fewer encampments is affirmed in research commissioned by the DETR/DTLR. This acknowledges that the biannual counts do not take into account the cycle that takes place within and between local authority areas on a daily and weekly basis; an ongoing shifting of largely the same people and same vehicles from one stopping place to another:

> The statistical information on unauthorised camping gathered through the Gypsy Count is inadequate as a tool for assessing need and planning services accordingly. While the 'snapshot' method has become popular in other fields (for example in enumerating the extent of rough sleeping) it is acknowledged to have significant flaws. In particular, the Gypsy Count figures provide no information on the movement of Gypsies and Travellers around the country, or the length of stay in different locations. (Cowan et al, 2001, p 72)

Despite apparent confidence in the validity of its data on, and its policies concerning, unauthorised encampments, the government does also appear to recognise the need for additional action. Lord Whitty attached a proviso to the aforementioned positive statement of belief in the status quo:

> However, we are taking further action to ensure that this long term trend continues … £17 million is to be made available over the next three years [2000-2003] for the refurbishment and improvement of the existing network of local authority sites … My Department is also about to commission research into the availability and condition of sites, including how they are managed, as a means of assessing the need for further sites, and a precursor to the next Spending Review. (DETR, 2000a)

The research into sites is being carried out by the same Birmingham University researcher whose work led to the *Good practice guide* on managing unauthorised encampments (DETR/Home Office, 1998); that guidance is currently under review. As at spring 2002, it is unclear whether the output of research will indeed be ready in time to 'inform' the next spending review. As will be briefly discussed in Chapter Six, conflict over the preferred approach to unauthorised encampments between different government departments can lead to piecemeal change or unqualified inactivity in this field of policy development. The status quo is, for the time being, preserved.

Loss of public pitches

The number of unauthorised encampments cannot have been reduced by recent programmes of public Gypsy site closures by local authorities. A limited TLRU research initiative, previously unpublished and undertaken at the request of a

DETR Minister, surveyed local authority Gypsy site closures in England between January 1995 and January 2000[6].

The overall changes to pitch numbers in the period were that 418 pitches were gained and 736 pitches lost. Therefore, assuming that there were 5,214 pitches on public sites in January 1995 as reported in the published counts, in January 2000 there were 318 fewer pitches (4,896) than when the 1994 Criminal Justice and Public Order Act had just come into force.

Most of the pitches gained became available during 1995/96, on new sites being built or existing sites being extended shortly after the legal changes and while money was still available to do so. Five authorities stated, in January or February 2000, that they were trying to build, or enable to be built, more sites, but that difficulties accessing finance were hampering this objective.

Reasons given for the loss of pitches included: that on some sites single pitches had been combined into double pitches to meet the needs of growing families; poor management; vandalism and fly-tipping; deterioration in standards due to lack of finance for upgrading; and transfer to private ownership (which does not include transfer to contracted-out management – sites so transferred are still owned by local authorities and deemed to be public sites). Additionally, one site (with 15 pitches) that had long been in private ownership had been misreported as a public site.

A number of observations were made by the local authority personnel interviewed by TLRU in early 2000, regarding sites and pitches generally. Some of the pitches that were available to live on were not in a condition in which it was desirable to live. Those sites that have a 'pick and choose' policy to new residents may at times be more peaceful sites on which to live, but this approach subverts the 'safety net' feature of the public site network, and so there may be more roadside families for this reason, as well as a lack of sufficient overall pitches. Around ten sites nationally were not under immediate threat of closure, but nonetheless the residents feel continually insecure and the future of the sites is uncertain. Several of these had closure averted or delayed only because of arbitrary interventions by concerned lawyers or public figures. At least one third of local authority interviewees stated that there was a long waiting list (between one to three years) for a pitch on one of their sites. A significant number noted that 'next generation' Gypsies and Travellers were living in housing because they could not get a pitch. (Two stated that many of the Travelling People in their area were living in housing by choice and had a long tradition of doing so, although probably not on a long-term basis.)

At January 2001, DETR figures stated that the number of local authority Gypsy sites was 328, a total of 5,116 pitches; this being a net increase of 59 pitches during 2000 and a net loss of three sites. The department added that these figures took into account gains of 44 pitches on existing sites and 128 pitches on six new or reopened sites. The figures also incorporated losses of 113 pitches on sites, nine of which had been closed during the year 2000.

The total number of pitches recorded by the DETR in January 2001, 5,116, is 220 higher than that collected through the TLRU study one year earlier. Although 172 new pitches were recorded as having become available during the period 2000/01, 113 were recorded by the DETR as lost, so there is still a significant discrepancy between the DETR and TLRU figures (the latter having been, in most cases, confirmed by two departments of each authority).

In addition to the closure of existing sites, new sites are no longer being developed. Only two respondent authorities to the TLRU costs survey mentioned site provision in any way other than to express the view that central government should reinstate some sort of funding or other mechanism to enable it. The 1994 legislation may have removed the duty on local authorities to provide sites for Gypsies, but they retained a power to provide such sites under the 1960 Caravan Sites and Control of Development Act. Few authorities have employed this discretionary power.

Some police officers believe that numbers of unauthorised encampments have increased in their area due to insufficient sites, and that this has placed additional strains on their resources in dealing with unauthorised encampments:

> We are still of the opinion that such legislation is primarily for Local Authorities to implement and enforce. Yet four years into the Act many have still to provide suitable designated sites. This situation has in our opinion contributed significantly to the problems associated with the current legislation. It is essential that adequate provision be provided for Travellers, together with their vehicles to camp in circumstances that are satisfactory to everyone ... We continue to maintain that this is a social problem in which the whole community has a part to play. Police intervention should be as a last resort when all other avenues have failed and only then when the full requirements of the legislation have been met.[7]

Regardless of the reasons for the numbers and causes of unauthorised encampments, a substantial number continue to take place each year, and concerns continue to be expressed by the statutory sector as to the costs associated with them. In a press release issued following the Annual General Meeting of the Chartered Institute of Environmental Health (London, 1 July 1998), the Institute stated its belief that:

> Besides being an attack on the lifestyle of a minority group, the Criminal Justice Act has created a 'merry-go-round' of evictions, moving the Travelling communities from one local authority to another. This has been financially wasteful and environmentally damaging. It is in everyone's interests – travellers, local residents and the Government – that we take a more compassionate approach.

Notes

[1] Since the introduction of the Race Relations (Northern Ireland) Order 1997, recognising Irish Travellers as an ethnic minority group protected within race relations legislation, powers of designation were deemed to breach such legislation and were thus rescinded.

[2] This assertion is in itself objectionable; 'cost-effectiveness' is not the basis of providing accommodation for homeless people; it is arguably the role of society to provide for the homeless, whether or not it is an economically profitable exercise.

[3] The quotations cited here are from correspondence to the DoE, which is archived and available for viewing at the ODPM, Eland House, Bressenden Place, London.

[4] The Association of District Councils noted in its response to the paper that this took place "without any prior consultation with the local authority associations or their members, and is considered ill-judged and premature, since it anticipates a change in existing legislation which has not yet come to pass".

[5] The official count ceased to take place in Wales from 1997. The justification given in Welsh Office correspondence was that there was no utility in collating figures when a duty to provide sites in respect of those figures no longer existed. The report *Traveller children and educational need in Wales* (Cardiff University School of Education, 1998) identified twice as many Travelling children in Wales than had the last governmental counts, approximately 2,000; and pointed out that many more Travelling children (such as those in housing) were also not included.

[6] Detailed figures can be provided on request from the TLRU; see www.cf.ac.uk/claws/tlru

[7] Letter to the TLRU from the Police Superintendents Association of England and Wales, 5 November 1998.

THREE

The costs to local authorities

Methodology

The research study that underscores this account was carried out via a postal survey of county, unitary, metropolitan, London borough and district councils in the UK, including Scotland and Northern Ireland (a total of 464 local authorities). Six central government agencies were also approached for information: the Crown Estate Commissioners, the Duchy of Lancaster, English Nature, Forest Enterprise, the Ministry of Agriculture Fisheries and Food, and the Ministry of Defence.

Both qualitative and quantitative data were sought (see Appendix C) and, in addition, respondents were encouraged to comment briefly on any specific issues which they believed had been raised by the questionnaire. The survey was aimed at highlighting how local authority and other public policies may differ, and to outline the implications for 'Best Value' in the context of the coming into force of the 1999 Local Government Act on 1 April 2000 (see further in Chapter Five).

The survey sought to assess total public authority expenditure relating to Travelling People. Authorities were asked how much money and other resources they had expended in the period 1 September 1998 to 31 August 1999, directly and indirectly, in 'dealing with' unauthorised encampments. The questions distinguished between estimated figures and audited figures. The survey then sought to assess the extent to which local authorities had attempted to audit this expenditure centrally (for instance as a form of 'Best Value' monitoring). The study also analysed categories of direct and indirect expenditure recorded by the authorities (and perhaps of equal importance, the types of expenditure not recorded)[1].

By way of example, direct and recordable costs could include legal fees, eviction costs, site clearance, engineering works to stop further encampments (fencing, ditching and so on) and planning enforcement costs. Indirect but potentially recordable costs could include officer time (not merely legal officers, but also highways, social services, Gypsy and Traveller Liaison, planning and education officers and others)[2].

Basic data

The overall response rate to the survey of 70% was remarkably high (varying from 81% of Scottish authorities to 62% in Northern Ireland). Of the English authorities, the response rate varied from 61% for district councils (145 of 237) and 75% for outer London authorities (15 of 20); the overall average also being 70%. In total, responses were received from 306 of the 464 local authorities in the UK to whom the TLRU questionnaire was sent. All percentages that follow are therefore not proportions of UK authorities as a whole but of respondent authorities.

Of all respondent authorities, 75% stated that they had incurred costs in respect of unauthorised encampments. However, significant variations existed; whereas 91% and 88% for English unitary and Welsh authorities respectively stated that they had incurred costs, only 11% of inner London authorities declared this to be the case.

The costs borne by local authorities in managing unauthorised encampments are likely to be a measure of the number of such encampments and their size. Accordingly authorities were asked to quantify, not only the number of unauthorised encampments in their area during the research period, but also the number of Travelling People living at these encampments. Seventy-two authorities had difficulty in assessing the number of people present at an encampment; a very few had difficulty in providing a precise number of caravans, and provided instead an estimate of the number of families involved. Of the 217 respondents who were able to give figures in answer to this question, 151 stated that they were only an estimation.

A total of 3,095 unauthorised encampments were reported for the period, 2,865 in England. The numbers of Travelling People involved were appraised, by those authorities that felt able to make such an estimate, at just over 35,000. (Some of these Travelling People, of course, may be the same people being recounted.)

There is little extant research concerning the occupancy rate of Gypsy and Traveller caravans or the size of Travelling families. A 1967 report by the Ministry of Housing and Local Government/Welsh Office suggested that the average Gypsy or Traveller household contained 4.5 persons or more and occupied on average one and a half 'units of accommodation' (Ministry of Housing and Local Government/Welsh Office, 1967, p 14). Almost ten years later, further research suggested that the average household size was slightly larger, at five persons, but it did not give an indicative figure for the caravan occupancy ratio at that time (Adams et al, 1975). Cripps also assessed family size as being between 4.5 and five (1976, p 8). While the report *Counting Gypsies* (Green and OPCS, 1991, p 31) was not directly concerned with this issue, it recorded local authority practice as estimating that there were five persons per family, and that families occupied between one and two caravans.

Analysing the TLRU questionnaire responses, therefore, where authorities have been unable to provide details of the number of people accommodated in a caravan, or where they were unable to provide a precise number of caravans stationed on an unauthorised encampment, the assumption has been made that one caravan = two persons, and one family = five persons.

If one discounts double counting between county and district councils (by removing from the calculation the figures for county councils), the results provide a rough average of almost ten unauthorised encampments per authority.

This calculation can be subjected to crude verification on the basis that the expected number of unauthorised encampments per county council would correspond to ten times the number of district councils it comprised; and, upon analysis, this appears to be broadly correct.

Unfortunately, the lack of sufficiently detailed data on site size and composition meant that no statistically significant conclusions could be drawn from this aspect of the survey. This is regrettable, since such information, if collected by local authorities, could be of considerable value; for instance, it could validate (or otherwise) the view that a few highly mobile groups of Travelling People cause a large proportion of the unauthorised encampments that result in significant authority expenditure.

There is no empirical reason why unauthorised encampments should inevitably result in local authorities incurring additional expenditure. Accordingly, the survey sought to establish the extent to which there is a link between these factors. Ideally, research might be able to establish a degree of proportionality between the number of unauthorised encampments, their size and composition, and the extent of the costs incurred by the local authority.

Only 5% of English authorities reported that they had borne no costs in relation to the unauthorised encampments within their area – although they were also able to provide information in respect of the numbers of unauthorised encampments and/or persons in their area in the period. In contrast, a surprisingly large number of Scottish authorities (35%) indicated that they had incurred no costs in relation to their unauthorised encampments. There is no clear evidence as to why this should be the case; the idea that it might be a function of Scotland's generally low population densities is not consistent with the evidence from Wales or Northern Ireland where all of the respondent authorities with unauthorised encampments reported consequential costs.

The evidence is therefore overwhelmingly to the effect that unauthorised encampments in virtually all areas of England, Wales and Northern Ireland directly result in some degree of local authority expenditure. (The position in Scotland is explored in a case study later in this chapter.)

Local and 'long-distance'

Forty-five percent of English authorities that responded to the question estimated that all of their costs were attributable to 'long-distance' Travelling People; 57 UK authorities in total stated this to be the case. Fifty-eight UK authorities believed 'long-distance' Travellers to be the cause of 80 to 99 percent of costs. Only 36 authorities considered that such Travellers accounted for less than 50% of total expenditure. (The survey defined 'long distance' as meaning 'Travellers who come to your area only once or twice a year and often only remain for relatively short periods'.) Therefore a significant number of respondents to the TLRU study did not feel that the Travelling People associated with unauthorised encampments in their areas were 'local people'.

There are two possible interpretations of statements about the 'long-distance' nature of people occasioning public expenditure on unauthorised encampments.

One is that a small number of highly mobile Travelling families are causing a significant proportion of the costs associated with unauthorised encampments. It is possible that this might be the case, particularly given that in the English Midlands-London corridor a few highly mobile families are known to pass through, often making a significant impact on their surroundings. However, the high number and geographical spread of this response suggests another interpretation. That is, that the Travelling People are not viewed as having significant 'local connections' or as forming part of the local (taxpaying) 'community'.

The statistically significant responses do add to the anecdotal evidence that a disproportionate amount of costly unauthorised encampments concern non-local Travelling People. If this is the case, then it is a trend that was first recorded by Cripps (1976, p 12), who noted that Gypsies were increasingly travelling in larger groups and that four large Irish groups had been identified.

Whether or not this is the case depends upon many factors, not least the ability of the respondents to differentiate between local and 'long-distance' Travellers. On the face of it, it appears likely that this is a skill local authorities would possess. For instance, in the 1991 report *Counting Gypsies* (Green and OPCS, paragraph 11.4), it is noted that Gypsy Liaison Officers did not consider there was a problem differentiating between local and transitory Travellers.

If the respondents have correctly identified the Travelling People in question, then the results are of significance and would warrant further research. It would indicate that either there has been a major shift in Travelling patterns since the 1991 report, or that unauthorised encampments created by 'long-distance' Travelling People are disproportionately expensive to manage. This proposition arose from the 1991 report, which noted that local authorities considered 73% of those on unauthorised sites to be 'settled' Travelling People and only 27% to be 'transitory'.

As noted, another possibility is that a majority of authorities see Travelling People as 'non-local', as not being members of the local citizenry, regardless of family ties or historical patterns of travel (facts of which some Gypsy and Traveller Liaison Officers may not be aware). This would carry implications for Travelling People in areas of policy and service provision where the 'local' has some definitional and determinative function, be it remedies for homelessness or other issues. These findings are highly relevant to the discussion of the implementation of the 'Best Value' programme by local authorities discussed further in Chapter Five.

In the case of a few respondents, this distinction as to 'local' and 'long-distance' extended to concerns about who paid the costs of unauthorised encampments as well as who was seen to create them. One English district council stressed to TLRU that it was local residents who paid the costs, rather than the council; stating that unauthorised encampments were a "totally unjustified burden on local Council tax payers, robbing them of services which could otherwise be provided".

Budgeting for and categorising costs

Local authorities were asked whether they operated a budget for some or all of the activity connected with unauthorised encampments and, if so, how much it was and from where it was managed. The majority of respondents with spending on encampments noted that they did not; only 26% of respondents and spending authorities reported having a dedicated budget for this.

Many authorities without a budget noted that monies for expenditure on encampment issues came from general departmental and/or contingency budgets. Of those spending authorities with a dedicated budget, these were located in a wide variety of departments, including: Development or Special Projects (2); Environmental Health or Services (20); Public Health (6); Estates (5); general budgets (that is, those of the relevant landowning department) (4); Housing (1); Legal (4); Leisure/Recreation (2); Planning (7); Policy (2); Property (3); and the Treasurer or Valuation department (2).

The lowest annual budget (an English district council) was £500, the highest (in an English metropolitan authority) £183,000. Only one budget was reported in each of Scotland and Northern Ireland (£4,000 and approximately £86,000 respectively). The average budget in England and Wales was just short of £19,000. A small minority of authorities who did not have costs associated with encampments during the period, nonetheless noted that they do have a budget on which to draw should the need arise. These contingency budgets are small, perhaps reflecting the sporadic nature of the issue in these areas: £18,500 among eight authorities.

The survey asked respondents to particularise their expenditure under six broad headings, namely 'legal', 'officer time', 'clearing up' and site 'protection', 'planning' and 'other'. Although it is inevitable that any attempt to compartmentalise expenditure into discrete groupings will create overlap problems, these particular categories (which were identified during the piloting of the survey questionnaire) appear to have been readily understood by the vast majority of respondents.

Legal costs

The combined legal costs reported by those authorities that responded to the survey amounted to over £625,000 for the one-year period. The costs were essentially broken down into 'disbursements' (that is, actual payments by the authority) and the costs of solicitor and officer involvement in the court process.

The recording of disbursements by an authority (including court fees, barrister fees, bailiff and inquiry agent fees, and so on) ought to be of a relatively high degree of reliability, since the information must be retained by the authority and is likely to be relatively easily accessible. In similar measure, legal department time records might be expected to be more accurate than general time recording for other departments. Many legal departments keep such records in order to be able to attribute the consequent costs to their authority's individual departments; in addition, by training, lawyers are inculcated with the discipline of time recording (since it is the principle measure by which charges are assessed).

The figures provided, however, would tend to suggest that legal departments have nonetheless under-recorded officer time. It is highly unusual in any proceedings for court fees to exceed the cost attributable to the time of solicitors and legal executives. However, as this research reveals, the costs of legal officer time combined amounted to approximately £130,000, whereas the court fees exceeded £153,000. The implication therefore is that, even in this domain, officer time is not always accounted for formally (nor, consequently, the cost to the authority of this activity).

Staff time

The attributable, non-legal staff costs reported to the TLRU are significant; exceeding £1.3 million in the study period. Few, if any, external sources are available to check whether these accurately reflect the true situation, since no equivalent research has ever been undertaken.

The local authority representatives with whom the data has been discussed consider that the relative proportions of expenditure are probably broadly correct. Thus, the social services involvement is generally low (Cemlyn, 1998) in comparison to that of the education services. Although very substantial amounts of health visitor and other health staff time is spent on visits to unauthorised encampments (Morris and Clements, 2001), the bulk of this expenditure will be borne not by local authorities but by National Health Service Trusts.

While the reported figures appear to bear an appropriately consistent proportionate interrelationship, it is difficult to establish whether they are also of the correct order of magnitude. The comments made by a number of the questionnaire respondents might suggest that these figures are an underestimate. (These comments appear in abbreviated form in Table 3.5.) They suggest that many authority activities (such as officer time in responding to complaints, in visiting unauthorised encampments and attending meetings, and so on) are particularly hard to quantify.

Comments made outside the research study also suggest that the reported figures are an underestimate. By way of example, a delegate to a seminar held by the TLRU (in London, July 2000) to discuss this research stated that the figures gathered by the TLRU were "a vast underestimate of the actual costs. Anyone who has ever been involved with unauthorised encampments, whether evicted or 'tolerated', knows the true costs of them". Many other delegates – all local authority officers – concurred.

Authorities were also asked whether they employed a Gypsy or Traveller Liaison Officer or equivalent and, if so, whether they would still engage such specialist service providers if there were significantly fewer (or no) unauthorised encampments in their area. Sixty-three (25%) of the English authorities had such officers and ten would not if the situation were different. In Northern Ireland, three did (19%), of which one would prefer not to; in Scotland, 11 (42%) would all be retained; in Wales, of three such officers (18%), two would be retained and one authority was unsure. In the majority of cases, such specialist staff would be retained because they also had responsibility for, or involvement with, the management of authorised (public) sites.

Clearing up

A press release issued by a Sussex local authority (7 July 1999) described the costs of clearing up unauthorised encampment sites, after residents have left or been made to leave, as:

> ... a perennial problem. Not only are the gypsies breaking the law, they also leave the authorities to clear the site of rubbish and debris. Illegally camped families cause a problem for the whole community. We need to seek a long-term solution to this problem. We will be meeting with [the] Borough Council, the police and the landowner in order to look at the options for the long term. We will then consult with local residents.

The clearing and repairing of land following encampment was said by respondent authorities to have cost £1,127,819 in the period. Of those respondents that suggested that costs associated with unauthorised encampments are increasing (108 of 306), 26 identified the ongoing growth as being directly linked to the increased costs of site clearance and cleaning. This might be because site residents leave more detritus; because more settled people use unauthorised encampments as an opportunity to 'fly-tip'; or because the real costs of such work have gone up. Thirteen respondents expressly stated that they do not consider unauthorised encampments themselves to be the 'problem' but rather the costs and tensions associated with clearing up after them. This may also have a knock-on effect on the level of complaints about unauthorised encampments and the call on resources (including officer time) in responding to them.

One respondent stated that the "cost of clearing up is gradually increasing; the Travellers have no incentive to take their rubbish with them". One long-term effect of unauthorised encampments resulting from lack of appropriate authorised sites may be increased numbers of Travelling People who have grown to feel disenfranchised and less inclined to reduce their impact on sites. Four local authority respondents to the study identified increased costs as stemming from a growth in 'antisocial' and 'criminal' behaviour and 'nuisance' associated with some unauthorised encampments.

It seems unlikely that the costs relating to the clearing up of former unauthorised encampment sites will reduce in the future unless and until the causes and incidence of unauthorised encampments themselves are controlled.

Site 'protection'

The figures gained from the TLRU study suggest that the 'protection' of 'vulnerable' sites has become a significant cost to local authorities. A sum of

£624,054 was said by UK authorities to have been expended on securing land against further encampments (such as ditching, fencing and so on) during the one-year period. A further £65,150 was spent on 'general precautionary measures' to prevent encampments from occurring and £29,350 on related unspecified activity.

These cost considerations include not only the cost of carrying out 'protection' works, but the value of such expenditure in effectively 'managing' unauthorised encampments. While anecdotal evidence suggests that some Travelling People can overcome protection works and 'break onto' such sites, therefore causing the need for further expenditure in respect of 'protecting' the same site, much of the work is effective in rendering the site unavailable for use by unauthorised encampments for the foreseeable future. It is possible, therefore, that these costs may not be increasing year on year, as more and more land becomes inaccessible for use as living space.

The government suggests that it may be appropriate for public landowners to take 'protection' action:

> Undertaking works to prevent access to land by Gypsies and Travellers so as to avoid unauthorised entry and encampment has an important role to play, especially in some urban areas. It may be urged on local authorities by the courts (where eviction orders are being sought repeatedly for the same site) or the police (where repeated encampment brings the fear of public order problems). It may also be urged on private landowners by local authorities – as in Northampton where the local authority will not take eviction action on behalf of a private landowner after two encampments if no protection works are undertaken. (DETR/Home Office, 1998, p 16)

However, while the *Good practice guide* is advising here that comprehensive programmes of land 'protection' could reduce encampments (as appears to have happened in its case study areas of Coventry and Northampton), it also immediately goes on to counsel that such protection "might shift Gypsies and Travellers elsewhere". Accordingly, the *Guide* recommends that the practicalities of site protection "should be carefully weighed. Not all sites can successfully be protected, and expenditure in unsuccessful works is wasted" (p 16).

A number of respondents to the TLRU survey had no doubt but that expenditure of this nature constituted value for money; one stated that most of its "problems were with unauthorised use of car parks. All car parks, since October 1998, have been protected with physical barriers to discourage Travellers. So far they have worked and we have been 'traveller-free' since then". It is possible, however, that such authorities may in consequence suffer unauthorised encampments on other (unsuitable) pieces of land in the longer term, or that neighbouring authorities might be dissatisfied with the results of this expenditure where unauthorised encampments are 'shifted' away from an area by protection works.

As noted, the 1998 Birmingham research acknowledged that site 'protection' may not reduce unauthorised encampments overall, but simply push them onto other pieces of land within or outside the local authority area. Additionally, more recent government-commissioned research notes that these ensuing unauthorised encampments may in consequence be more problematic in nature. "Traditional sites that may have been used by groups of Gypsies and Travellers for generations have been redeveloped, and public and private land, that has been used in previous years, is being 'protected' from incursions. All of this forces Gypsies and Travellers onto sites that may be less suitable and more visible" (Cowan et al, 2001, p 72). According to the English counts (and 43 respondents to this study), unauthorised encampments are not reducing over time. It seems likely therefore that any savings resulting from 'protection' by an authority in the short term may result in additional expenditure on unauthorised encampments on other sites in the area or by other local authority areas to which unauthorised encampments move as a result.

While 24 TLRU respondents attributed a decrease in unauthorised encampment-related costs to site protection, and nine to development of former unauthorised encampment sites, seven identify these actions as increasing such costs. A further seven authorities note that the carrying out of protection works itself has increased costs, and three suggest that non-toleration policies and/or site protection on the part of neighbouring local authorities has inflated their expenditure.

The costs associated with the 'protection' of 'vulnerable' sites identified in the TLRU research project are substantial, and are likely to represent a considerable underestimate. Reasons for this shortfall include: inadequate recording of expenditure; that 30% of authorities did not respond to the study; and that much capital expenditure occurred prior to the period of the survey (but the results of which will have nevertheless impacted on the costs of unauthorised encampments for the period).

Considerable evidence exists (external to this survey) of such costs; for instance, a September 2000 media report which highlighted that the London Borough of Hillingdon had completed the first phase of a £250,000 programme to stop unauthorised encampments by putting in gates and barriers at entrances to 39 open spaces (*Uxbridge, Ruislip and Northwood Times*, 30 September 2000). The programme followed a pilot scheme in 1998, when ten sites were 'protected' at a cost of £25,000. The newspaper article noted that the expenditure would have a substantial impact on the future costs of unauthorised encampments, both in that Borough and in neighbouring areas.

Site protection, and the consequent decrease in available sites on publicly owned land, may result in what one respondent described as "an increased tendency by Travelling People to move onto private land, which is a significant burden for a land-owner" (the potential cost implications for private landowners are explored further in the following chapter). The comments by respondents at the end of this chapter demonstrate that the effect on private landowners is a feature of the site protection process; one simply stated that unauthorised encampments were "not our problem". Twelve respondents said that their encampment-associated costs had decreased due to the 'problem' being dealt with by (or in liaison with) private landowners. However, this is likely to have the indirect impact of increasing the costs associated with 'public' complaints to local authorities, as at least some such complainants will be private landowners or their neighbours.

As to who benefits from site protection, aside from those local authorities that report a subsequent decrease in the costs of unauthorised encampments, it is obvious that firms providing goods and services in relation to 'protection' of land from unauthorised encampments are likely to be profiting. In 1998 one 'street furnishing services' company was charging between £75 and £350 per 'access denial system' permanent unit (that is, a pyramidal roadblock), depending on size, weight and finish[3].

Planning and other costs

Costs related to planning functions are not as relevant for county councils as they are for other types of authority. Planning costs can include the legal costs of enforcement action (such as notices and injunctions), which were said to total £14,000; officer costs for dealing with enforcement appeals and related duties (£20,600); costs relating to planning enforcement following notices (£3,500); and other unspecified costs (£8,100). A total of £89,400 was said by respondents to have been expended on planning-related matters in the period.

Other miscellaneous costs, not related to any of the broad headings outlined previously, can include compensation paid to local landowners; officer time and travel for special engagements, such as specialist conferences and regional statutory and voluntary sector meetings; officer time spent attending planning disputes; and liaison with the media on encampment issues. Expenditure on such activities was said by respondent UK authorities to have cost £51,099 in the period.

These sums are not considerable in the context of overall spending in relation to unauthorised encampments, but nonetheless are probably significant in small authorities with small budgets, and again represent an underestimate. The majority of respondents did not give data under these headings, not necessarily because such expenditure was not made, but because it has not been formally counted.

'Toleration'

Some responses to the TLRU survey suggest that recommended 'good practice' can be expensive. Both the *Good practice guide* and DoE and Welsh Office Circular 18/94 (1994a) (which accompanied the 1994 CJPOA) advise that unauthorised encampments should be 'tolerated' as long as there is no intolerable nuisance associated with them (that is, an appropriate length of stay negotiated with site residents). The guidance also suggests that local authorities might provide services to the unauthorised encampment, such as toilets, skips or water.

Eight respondents to this study stated that the eviction process is now more costly and complicated; four that the adoption of a 'toleration' policy has itself increased expenditure and/or resulted in an expensive 'honey-pot' effect (the principle being that Travelling People are naturally drawn to more tolerant areas). Two asserted that *Good practice guide* and/or 1998 Human Rights Act considerations (see further in Chapter Six) have increased costs. Six identify 'toleration' as occasioning a decrease in costs, but most appear to 'sense' this rather than being able to point to hard data to buttress their view. (The sole respondent who could empirically prove toleration to have decreased costs is examined more closely as a case study in Chapter Five.)

Some authorities have expressed concern elsewhere that neighbouring, less tolerant, authorities will pass on costs:

> Due to the non-toleration policies of surrounding councils, there are more encampments in this area. The gypsy community is aware of the attitude of local authorities to encampments. Word is quick to travel amongst the community; therefore to tolerate a single encampment may open the floodgates. Other families may enter Council land illegally and claim that the Council has an implied policy of allowing gypsy encampments citing the [Gypsy family name], so long as they remain, as an illustration. If this precedent was to develop, it would become increasingly difficult to defend valuable land from occupation and would involve the Council in continuing expenditure to recover possession of land. Furthermore a sudden influx of gypsy groups to industrial areas would make marketing vacant land and buildings increasingly difficult and prospective occupiers would look elsewhere. (Director of Environmental Services, an English borough council, 1999)

A respondent to this research stated that the 'toleration' of unauthorised encampments can be expensive:

> The bulk of costs are spent in dealing with complaints, which increase with the length of time an encampment remains. Therefore toleration would perhaps increase costs. For example, in April 1997 a large group of 22 adults and 27 children, with a woman in the later stages of pregnancy, were 'tolerated' for 21 days, thus increasing the cost to the authority.

Another respondent authority considered its perceived decrease in unauthorised encampments to be 'a question of luck'.

It appears that some authorities do not accept the official view outlined in Chapter One (in the section on the nature of unauthorised encampments) that speedier evictions can lead to more encampments. These authorities see speed of action as appropriate and beneficial, for example one respondent stated that their "policy speeds up [the] eviction process. Current removal time 3 days". Some authorities stated that they might adopt such a policy should they experience any unauthorised encampments, although they acknowledge the potential futility of such an approach: "[This] Council has been fortunate in recent years by having no real gypsy or traveller encampments ... of course, these people have to live somewhere and every time they are moved on, they become someone else's problem".

The 'zero tolerance' approach to unauthorised encampments has long run contrary to government guidance, on grounds that include consideration of costs of all kinds, be they financial, human or social:

> The Secretaries of State recognise that in some situations it may be essential to move gypsies; they also accept that it may be reasonable to fence off some sites from which gypsies have moved voluntarily. However, they do not accept that it is ever necessary to operate a general and indiscriminate policy of eviction. The Departments have always taken the opportunity to remind local authorities of the human misery as well as the considerable waste of time and financial resources and the increased pressures on neighbouring authorities caused by the indiscriminate eviction of gypsies from illegal encampments when there is no space available for them on an authorised site. (DoE and Welsh Office, 1978)

Nonetheless, a few authorities told the TLRU that, regardless of whether it is cost-effective to move people on or of the effect on neighbouring areas, it is "what local people want". For instance, one respondent had "recently employed a zero tolerance policy utilising self-help under common law, requiring that travellers leave authority land within 24 hours of notice served. We have had fewer encampments utilising this method".

Measured, unmeasured and immeasurable costs

Certain costs are difficult to identify and quantify (some of these are referred to by respondents in the comments in Table 3.5). Those respondents that had experienced unauthorised encampments in the period were asked whether they had recorded the financial costs borne in responding to these encampments to any degree. Only 68 of 229 authorities with spending in the period had recorded any details of such expenditure. (Additionally, eight authorities in England and two in Scotland that had not incurred costs in respect of encampments during the period noted that they do usually record such costs as and when they arise.)

A significant number of respondents stated that they were unable to quantify costs accurately in relation to some defined categories such as officer time spent at special meetings, liaison with the media, and so on. Out of 306 respondent authorities, 136 were unable to estimate unauthorised encampment costs at all, although they were aware that site visits, meetings with local residents, telephone calls, correspondence, media liaison and so on had all been associated with unauthorised encampments in their areas.

Some respondents saw particular costs as being relevant to this research and therefore reported them, whereas others did not, even if they had incurred such expenditure. By way of example, a Scottish rural council included the costs of employing a Community Development Officer and Travellers Site Manager in its assessment, in addition to an annual payment made to a voluntary organisation for services provided. Although it periodically had to evict

Travelling People from unauthorised encampments, and resorted to the police service at these times, it could not give any costing for such action.

Eighteen respondent English authorities that stated that they had incurred no costs during the period had, according to the DETR Gypsy counts for January and July 1999, experienced significant numbers of unauthorised encampments: 357 caravans in total on both of those single days combined. Four respondent authorities stated that they had borne no costs in relation to unauthorised encampments, and yet could state that they had experienced at least 22 in the period; it is likely that in fact at least some resources were expended in respect of these unauthorised encampments, if only to gather such information.

Those respondents that recorded such costs were asked to quantify them using a table attached to the questionnaire (see Appendix C). A slightly revised version (to allow for totals) containing overall UK totals appears as Table 3.1. The figures include those given by authorities that do not formally record the costs associated with unauthorised encampments, but felt able to offer a 'guesstimate' of what they had spent in relation to unauthorised encampments during the period 1 September 1998 to 31 August 1999.

Several points should be borne in mind with reference to these tables:

- Again, it should be noted that 136 of 306 respondents could not provide any information as to costs.
- Some authorities record the costs of unauthorised encampments but did not feel able, or were not willing, to provide any information about the detail of these costs.
- Some authorities do not record the costs and yet felt able to provide estimated information about their expenditure on unauthorised encampments.
- The sectional totals are less than the overall total figure by £401,350; this is because some authorities were unable to break down costs in any detail but could attribute a figure to the sectional and/or final totals.
- It is certain that some of the authorities that did not respond to this research incurred costs relating to unauthorised encampments during the period, as more than 50 such authorities are recorded as having experienced unauthorised encampments in the biannual count undertaken by the DETR.
- As has been noted, a total of 3,095 unauthorised encampments were reported for the period, 2,865 in England. This is only slightly more than English authorities alone were officially recorded as having experienced on a single day during the period (see Table 2.2). That even the official counts are regarded as an underestimation suggests that the numbers reported through the TLRU survey are a miniscule proportion of the true incidence of encampments, and therefore of the costs associated with them.

Table 3.1: Breakdown of annual costs: UK total

Legal costs (*planning is separate;* *see below*)	Court fees	£155,646
	Officer time in attending court proceedings	£58,485
	Counsel fees	£36,376
	Solicitor time	£81,971
	Bailiff fees	£109,315
	Inquiry agents/process servers	£29,070
	Hire of removal vehicles	£31,200
	Other	£53,256
	Total	**£682,954**
Attributable staff costs (*ie,* *costs of officer time spent* *working in relation to* *encampments*)	Gypsy/Traveller Liaison Officer(s)	£377,845
	Social services	£14,650
	Health	£15,100
	Education	£448,282
	Environmental health	£200,391
	Highways	£40,687
	Providing facilities for encampment(s) (ie, water, toilets, refuse collection, etc, for which no charge is made)	£138,023
	Other	£150,385
	Total	**£1,435,792**
Building works	Clearing and repairing land following encampment	£1,127,819
	Securing against further encampments (ie, ditching, fencing, etc)	£624,054
	General precautionary measures to prevent encampments from occurring	£65,150
	Other	£29,350
	Total	**£1,657,528**
Planning (*the authors are aware that* *planning may be less* *relevant for county councils*)	Legal costs of enforcement action (ie, notices, etc)	£14,000
	Officer costs for dealing with enforcement appeals, etc	£20,600
	Costs relating to planning enforcement following notices	£3,500
	Other	£8,100
	Total	**£89,400**
Other	For example, compensation paid to local landowners; officer time and travel for special meetings; officer time spent attending planning disputes; liaison with media, etc	**£51,099**

Total £4,318,123

Increasing and decreasing costs

Respondents to the survey were asked whether they believed that the annual costs of responding to unauthorised encampments are increasing or decreasing. Of 306 authorities, 108 believe them to be increasing, 78 to be decreasing, 57 believe them to be static, nine feel that they vary too much year on year to make such an estimation, and 54 were unsure. The reasons given for such answers are outlined in the following tables ('UEs' refers to unauthorised encampments). Seventy-two respondent authorities did not answer the question, could not be sure of the answer, or answered 'n/a' (not applicable) as they had apparently experienced no unauthorised encampments in the period.

Additional comments

Respondents were given the opportunity to make any comments they wished in relation to unauthorised encampments and costs generally, and 73 of 306 chose to do so. The figures in the following tables represent the number of UK authorities who made each statement.

Table 3.2: Costs are perceived to be increasing

Costs are increasing because:	Number
More unauthorised encampments / Travellers generally	43
Increase in refuse / vandalism / clean-up / fly-tipping costs	26
Increase in employment costs / time / changes in public funding	15
More complaints from settled community / council members	14
Increase in use of courts / legal and court costs	12
Larger groups travelling together / remaining for longer	12
Travellers appear more able / likely to challenge legal action	10
Eviction process now more costly / complicated	8
Development / protection of former UE sites	7
Increased costs in 'protecting' sites	7
Inflationary increase in all associated costs generally	6
Increase in Traveller population / site need generally	5
Inflation in costs / use of contractors	5
Adoption of 'toleration' policy / 'honey-pot' effect	4
Increased antisocial / criminal behaviour / nuisance	4
Shortage / closure of authorised sites	4
Action in respect of same groups on different sites	3
Non-toleration / site protection by neighbouring authorities	3
UEs now more likely on more 'visible' public / private land	3
Failure by police / other agencies to use powers	2
Good practice guide / Human Rights Act considerations	2
Increased number of children being directed to schools	2
New land bought / transferred from other bodies	2
More time negotiating with people on encampments	1
Provision of services to unauthorised encampments	1

Table 3.3: Costs are perceived to be decreasing

Costs are decreasing because:	Number
'Protection' of sites on which UEs formerly took place	24
Fewer unauthorised encampments / Travellers generally	16
'Problem' dealt with by / liaison with private landowners	12
Provision / improvement of authorised sites by this authority	12
'Rigorous' / 'robust' eviction / enforcement procedures	12
Development of sites on which UEs formerly took place	9
Increased use / adoption of 'toleration' policy	6
Adoption of non / zero toleration policy	4
Increased involvement by other type of authority	4
Increased adoption of housing by Travellers	3
More robust approach by police	3
Better liaison between authorities and police	2
Increased liaison with people on unauthorised encampments	2
'Luck'	2
Provision of authorised sites by other authorities	2
Travellers move of own accord before action taken	2
Communication of robust approach through Gypsy community	1
Fewer long-distance Travellers	1
'Immediate local concern'	1
Interagency working	1
Local socio-economic issues	1

Table 3.4: Costs are perceived to be stable

Costs remain stable because:	Number
Increases only caused by annual / one-off events	5
Not really a problem	4
Same Travellers; unwilling to settle on public site	3
Balanced by fewer UEs but more intolerant local residents	2
Geographical features of the area	2
Communication of robust approach through Gypsy community	1
Cost limited to contacting landowners to arrange 'move on'	1
Few want to stay permanently in our area	1
More UEs but speedier management procedures	1
Most work done by another authority	1
'Rigorous' / 'robust' eviction / enforcement procedures	1
Some sites expensive to clean up, some not	1
Toleration policy	1
Travellers move on as soon as legal process started	1

Table 3.5: Additional comments by respondents

Comment	Number
UEs not the problem but site clearance; costs and tensions	13
The costs to private landowners are unaccounted for	8
Legislation to enable speedy removal would reduce costs	5
Local people feel we should act more quickly to remove UEs	5
Civil possession proceedings are long-winded and expensive	4
Short-term toleration / interagency working seems to save money	4
A government decision on site provision would reduce costs	3
Costs of responding to complaints difficult to quantify	3
Increasingly costs are related to clearing up sites after UEs	3
Not a cost-effective way of spending large sums of money	3
Costs are hardly ever recovered from the people on the UEs	2
Costs escalate enormously where large-scale UEs	2
Costs of visiting and investigating UEs difficult to quantify	2
Government has left authorities to cope with insoluble problem	2
Hidden costs: time spent attending meetings and lobbying	2
Increasingly costs are administrative / complaint management	2
Local concerns and resentment of UEs are high	2
Loss of officer time responding to complaints considerable	2
More transit sites are needed, although difficult to manage	2
No-one is happy and little is achieved by constant 'moving on'	2
Surprising authority cannot / it should quantify costs of UEs	2
The survey does not account for lost amenity / annoyance	2
Would be more sensibly dealt with on a county / regional basis	2
Authority dilemma: not knowing future UEs and the costs	1
Authority dilemma: 'tolerating' *and* protecting environment	1
'By-ways' Open to All Traffic' (BOTATs) cannot be protected	1
Costs affected by welfare needs at the particular UE	1
Debates as to which authority is responsible for clearance	1
Deliberate waste dumping should be monitored / charged for	1
Districts pay the real costs of a county council toleration policy	1
Eviction difficult to justify to courts and Travellers since 1994	1
Expenditure incurred for each UE curtailed with use of section 61	1
Guidance on 'toleration' is weak and subjective [Scotland]	1
Gypsy Liaison Officers need more support and role definition	1
Hidden costs to services involved with UEs, ie education	1
Human Rights Act will reduce costs to business / community	1
If the UE is on council land, legal action costs can be high	1
It should be lawful for assets to be seized until costs are paid	1
Long-term solutions are being explored, ie liaison with media	1
May reduce costs by restricting sites' commercial productivity	1
Members are firmly attached to a 'non-toleration' policy	1
Moved UEs just become someone else's problem	1

Table 3.5: Additional comments by respondents (contd.../)

Comment	Number
People have to live somewhere	1
Pitches on permanent sites are all taken up	1
Removal does not affect clean-up costs; size of UE does	1
Robust policies work but are expensive, ie bailiffs' costs	1
Significant police time spent working with the council	1
Site building reduces costs: 'invest to save'	1
Some UEs may involve the same people on different sites	1
The authority claims to make enquiries, but in practice no toleration	1
The *Good practice guide* has increased costs / officer time	1
The notion of romantic Romanies is gone; all seen as no good	1
There is no government recognition of the costs councils bear	1
Toleration increases costs as it leads to more complaints	1
Toleration will be at the expense of social disruption	1
Travelling is a parasitic lifestyle	1
UEs are getting larger: strength in numbers against authorities	1
Unjustified burden on taxpayers, robbing them of services	1

Case study: the costs in Scotland

In December 1999, Save the Children Fund (SCF) Scotland and the University of Dundee published a report, *Moving targets*, concerning unauthorised encampments in Scotland and the stance of local authorities towards them. It also examined "the experiences of over fifty Travelling families on the social effects on family life when they are required to move on, giving particular consideration to health care and children" (Morran et al, 1999, p 1). As the SCF report notes, in 1978 the Secretary of State's Advisory Committee on Scotland's Travelling People reported that "because of a lack of legal places to stay and forced 'moving on', the movement of a Traveller family in Scotland is more frequent than that resulting naturally from the pursuit of a livelihood by the parents" (Advisory Committee on Scotland's Travelling People, 1978, p 19).

The 1999 SCF report concluded that the issues facing Travellers on roadsides and other unauthorised encampments are part of a much wider socio-legal context in Scotland. "Our investigation shows that much of the motivation behind the policies and practices relating to Travellers is based on this ethnic minority being viewed as a 'problem' for which a 'solution' must be found. Until that attitude is challenged Travellers are likely to remain one of the most excluded groups in society" (Morran et al, 1999, p 1).

There has never been a statutory duty on Scottish local authorities to provide sites for Travellers; they are merely 'encouraged' to work towards a 'pitch target' set by the Scottish Office through any means, including public and private provision. Previous SCF research has suggested that targets may be set too low and that private sites are often not available to or are denied to Travellers (SCF, 1998). A predictable and actual consequence of this shortfall, as assessed by the SCF research, is the existence of more unauthorised encampments and more 'moving on'.

None of the Travelling families interviewed for the 1999 SCF study had moved on by their own choice. Eleven percent had moved because of fears for their own safety and other pressures from local communities; 66% because of actions by the police and/or local authorities and/or landowners. The research showed "no correlation between the Toleration Policy and the length of time Travellers were allowed to stay. There were numerous instances in areas covered by the Toleration Policy where families were told to move on immediately" (Morran et al, 1999, p 6).

The report included details of five months in the life of one Travelling family in the Edinburgh area, showing the frequency, and therefore the frequency of costs, relating to the movements of a single Travelling unit (Morran et al, 1999, p 11; see Table 3.6).

SCF Scotland responded to a draft of the TLRU survey of costs, expressing concern about the incomplete picture presented in respect of Scotland. SCF questioned the accuracy of the costs provided by the Scottish local authority respondents; it considered that the costs claimed by the authorities presented a very substantial underestimate and highlighted in particular the "absence of legal costs". SCF also questioned the reported costs for precautionary building work, stating that it "regularly witnessed the establishment of 'state of the art' fencing and bouldering to prevent further encampments. As many Travellers say it seems to be the only council department that can appear at all hours and no expense spared".

By way of comparison, SCF made the following comments, based on its experience with a particular urban authority in Scotland; an authority that was not a respondent of the TLRU costs survey.

> Over the past year in this area there have been in excess of thirty unauthorised, or roadside camps, about a third of which have been on land owned by the council. The duration of all the camps has ranged from a few hours to several

Table 3.6: Travelling family in the Edinburgh area

Nature of site ownership	Period of stay	Reason for move
Public	1 month	Legal action
Private	36 hours	Restricted access
Private	8 hours	Farmer threats
Public	4 weeks	Legal action
Public	3 weeks	Legal action
Private	3 weeks	Legal action
Private	2 weeks	Personal choice
Public	4 weeks	Legal action

weeks and the same location has been used on more than one occasion. The costs are difficult to predict but if one considers one camp which was used for about four weeks and from which the occupiers were evicted following successful court action potential costs totalled £58,000 as follows:

Estimated legal costs (including court fees): £5,000

Estimated officer time dealing with complaints/offering advice: £3,000

Clean up costs (as advised by environmental service) £50,000.

It is worth pointing out, firstly, that the relevant Council has not met its pitch target and hence during the period covered the toleration policy was in operation and should have been applied; and secondly, that extremely limited services are provided on roadside camps. Water is not provided and refuse collection is done on a limited and sporadic basis. Rights advice and educational support are provided by Save the Children Fund and the council's Traveller Project respectively.

The breakdown of annual costs in Scotland as reported to the TLRU during its survey were: legal costs, £1,440; staff costs, £57,148; building works, £15,400; and planning and other costs, £3,200: a total of £77,188. If the figures provided by SCF are reasonably accurate, their total for a single encampment comes close to the combined costs of the 15 respondent local authorities in Scotland. This again suggests that the figures produced in the TLRU survey may materially under-record the total UK local authority expenditure on unauthorised encampments.

In 1999 the Advisory Committee on Scotland's Travelling People explained why the pitch target and site-building grant policy had been established in 1997. "It was recognised that where there is a shortfall in proper provision for Travellers, it is a waste of police, court and local authority resources to move Travellers from one unauthorised site to another" (1999, paragraph 5.1). It would appear that these schemes are also not proving effective and costs can consequently be considerable for all concerned, in some parts of Scotland at least. These conclusions are not immediately obvious from the relatively modest sums gathered by the TLRU in respect of Scotland, but evidently can be independently supported.

Totalling the costs

An annual figure of approximately £6 million expended on unauthorised encampments is almost certainly a substantial underestimate. The conclusion reached about underestimation following this survey is the same as that reached following the TLRU pilot research on the issue.

The local authorities that provided estimates of their costs failed to take into account (or to fully account for) staff time. Most have also failed to include the substantial costs of site clearance and engineering or building works to secure land against re-entry. Those local authorities that have taken some or all of these factors into account record significantly higher costs, at least 100% higher. It is therefore almost certain that the total figures in Table 3.1 are a significant undervalue of the true sum spent nationally in respect of unauthorised encampments during the period.

The figures in Table 3.1 represent only those costs counted by those authorities that responded to the research, and only those costs that they are able to count. And yet those figures are substantial in themselves. Of 306 respondents to this study, 108 stated their belief that these costs are increasing; 43 that the numbers of unauthorised encampments themselves are growing; and 57 that the costs, at best, remain the same. And the expenditure appears even more substantial when the relatively modest figures of the estimated Travelling populations are taken into account. Based on the biannual 'Gypsy' counts, if there are an average of 2,800 caravans on unauthorised encampments on any one day in the year, each caravan is costing landowners, public or private, at least £9 per day every day of the year (£9,000,000 ÷ 356 days = £25,280.90 per day ÷ 2,800 caravans = £9.03 approximately).

The costs are considered by some to be not only considerable and ongoing, but wasted:

> Since Travellers constantly move on, the number of separate encampments in any year is likely to be consistent (in 1997 Hillingdon had 45 and in 1998, 54). Rapid eviction proceedings may exacerbate the situation by leading to a large number of smaller encampments which places a strain on limited Council resources. This also provokes a hostile public reaction. The next site adopted may be less appropriate than the one vacated and may not even be outside the borough. "The Problem" can therefore never be solved but only moved on. In the absence of a wider national strategy towards Travellers as a whole, the most that can be achieved is shifting people from one site to another to no-one's advantage other than to spread and therefore equalise the public perception of nuisance. (London Borough of Hillingdon and the Metropolitan Police, 1999, para 2.6)[4]

It is not the purpose of this research to quantify the total financial costs to society of there being inadequate accommodation for Travelling People. However, it is clear that the figure of £6 million, derived from the respondent's data, represents a significant underestimate, although the survey parameters make it impossible to predict with accuracy the extent of this underestimate.

The evidence suggests that:

- The 30% of authorities that failed to respond are likely to have expenditure not dissimilar to the 70% that did.
- Respondent authorities materially underestimated their costs of managing unauthorised encampments.

- Other governmental and national agencies (such as the Highways agencies, the National Trust, railway operators, the Forestry Commission and other large landowning bodies) are likely to incur significant costs in managing unauthorised encampments on their land.
- The costs to private landowners and police are likely to be equally substantial, particularly as public bodies take ever greater site protection measures.

It is probably safe to assume that the actual figure of £6 million derived from this research could be multiplied a number of times before the real annual cost of managing unauthorised encampments is reached.

More importantly, however, these costs take no account of the social or human costs associated with inadequate accommodation for Travelling People (costs that are explored further in the following chapter). In 1988 Mr Justice Henry (as he then was) referred to this aspect of the costs equation in the following terms:

> If there are not sufficient sites where Gypsies may lawfully stop, then they will be without the law whenever and wherever they stop. This will result either in them being harried from place to place, or in them being allowed to remain where they should not lawfully be ... the social damage caused by there not being sufficient sites to accommodate the nation's Gypsies goes beyond the obvious effect of homelessness on the families concerned and on the conscience of the community.... Their plight will or should be an affront to the national conscience. (*R v Hereford and Worcester County Council ex parte Smith* [1998], cited in OSCE, 2000, p 117)

Notes

[1] The hard data on which these analyses and assertions are founded are, for the most part, too dry and demanding of space to be included in this publication. Tables are available on e-mail request to tlru-l@cf.ac.uk

[2] Although district councils were asked the same questions as other types of authority, due to their differing roles they place greater emphasis on the direct and indirect planning enforcement and environmental health costs they bear, and might omit answers concerning social worker and education officer time.

[3] The company's listed selling points are "no caravans, no trailers, no tipping, no costly clean-up, no unhappy general public, no unsightly parkland, no constant system repair/ replacement, no counting the cost of incursion". Information provided by Kent County Council.

[4] The borough spent £250,000 on site protection in 1999.

FOUR

The costs to others

The TLRU survey did not extend to police forces, private landowners, businesses and Travelling People. Although the costs to these sectors are likely to be considerable, little attempt has been made by researchers to quantify them. However, some information from primary and secondary sources reviewed during the course of the research is available, and provides some idea of the nature and scale of costs that may sometimes be involved.

Travelling People

Some of the many financial and human costs to Travelling children and adults that follow have been identified by Travelling People themselves or their service providers, in conversation with a TLRU researcher (references are given for other sources).

Midway between the introduction of the site provision duty and its repeal, the government published *The accommodation needs of long-distance and regional Travellers* (DoE, 1982), a consultation paper. Included within this paper was the following comment made by a 'long-distance' Traveller:

> We just go round and round like a game of dominoes and things are getting worse. Even getting onto a bit of land is difficult. We go round in a convoy and sometimes we get 10-15 of us on the bit of land and the Police come and stop the rest of us getting on. There's a lot of argument then and sometimes we all get on but it's bad if we don't, as the others have to go on the roadside.

> Then when we get onto the land the Police will be onto us. Sometimes they dig a trench all round with JCB diggers and say we can't get off unless we take our caravans with us. Well, we're trapped then. Can't take out cars to get food even and we can't get out to work. Then they will come into our trailers and ask for receipts for all the stuff there. Might have to go 100 miles back to the shop to get a receipt for the television, for example, and what do you do about the Crown Derby you've been given for the wedding? And there was one morning at 6 o'clock when they had warrants to search for firearms and we were all out of the trailers standing in a row while they searched. Tore the carpet up as well....

> Once we have overcome this initial police harassment which lasts a few days, we wait for the eviction order. And waiting for that is not easy. The men have to be careful not to leave when they might come and tow the trailers away. Sometimes people are ill: one time they hitched up a trailer and the midwife

looked out and said that a baby was going to be born. Other times people are in hospital. Some authorities allow us to stay then but sometimes they don't and then it's difficult with these family problems as well.

Everybody nearby objects at first and we have an uneasy friendship with the shops and pubs. The local people we don't see directly but a few have waved sticks at us when we try to get on to a bit of land but that's not important. The worst is what the papers say about us. People panic automatically when we first arrive and too much is written in the papers to frighten people against us. As they say, if a fox steals a hen, then a gypsy did it. After a few weeks things settle down and just when things are getting friendly we have to move out. (DoE, 1982, Appendix 3)

Psychological and practical problems

It is evident from this experience that the costs to Travelling People of unauthorised encampments, that is, of a lack of secure and lawful stopping places, are considerable and can take many forms. There is no evidence to suggest that the situation has improved by the passage of time since that account was written. A more recent account by a 13-year-old Scottish Traveller about life 'on the move' illustrates this point:

[S]ometimes you get moved twice in a week, other times you get to stay two or three weeks, the longest was when we got two months over Christmas. It would be nice to have somewhere to go after travelling in the summer, when you're getting shifted all the time the men can't look for work and you can't be spending on diesel all the time. When the police come on the camp they harass you, check the trailer and motor, look for stolen gear and some just don't listen and can be right cheeky. Others are alright and just say look we've a job to do, it's not us. Sometimes it's the locals too, if we've been there a while they might threaten to burn us out or chuck stones at the trailer. If you get shifted you have to miss school or going on the trips – you plan them, decide where to go and then you get moved. (Morran et al, 1999, p 11)

The disruption to the children of Travelling families during the process of eviction from unauthorised encampments is an issue that is widespread. Research by the Children's Society noted that eviction may bring about different feelings in children depending on how an eviction is carried out. Where people are given notices of eviction and then take a decision to move on themselves, there are feelings of loss for the children and perhaps too the adults. Where people are moved on by force, there can be feelings of fear.

Where a site had been established for a while children were leaving an area which was their home. Links that had been made with the local community were severed such as friendships made at school. Sites when they move on are often dispersed so that friendships made with other children and adults on site are disrupted.

A forced eviction can be a threatening and frightening experience for children. There is a fear of someone taking your parent away, taking your home away or of people that you care about being hurt. Even if the threat is more perceived than real, for children the involvement of force or coercion into the eviction process can be very frightening. (Children's Participation Project, 1998, p 12)

One Traveller woman told the TLRU that "you get no privacy. Anyone can march up to you while you're sat on the side of the road, anyone at all. Usually the police".

Repeated eviction, which leaves few opportunities to stop for any length of time, will naturally deny children sustained or even any access to mainstream education. One concern that many Travelling parents have is that, if children do get to school, an eviction may occur while children are there. Children may go to school with the fear that their parents will have been moved to another location when they return from school in the evening. (Added fears about rapid evictions are therefore likely to restrict children's attendance in some cases.)

The Children's Participation Project has also discussed the relationship between children, eviction and play. The Project points out that play forms an essential part of the social, physical and emotional development and learning of children, but that a safe place to play can be a rare treat for many Travelling children. "The inadequate number of sites provided for travellers and the preventative measures taken to stop access to traditional stopping places has forced families to stop in places where the external environment is not conducive to a safe playspace" (1998, p 5).

Earlier research by the Children's Society had expressed concern about the likely impact on children and families of increased evictions under the 1994 Criminal Justice and Public Order Act. The list of possible hardships listed by the Society included that, in the middle of winter, the cold, mud and lack of daylight meant gathering wood and water and maintaining vehicles was hard even on stable sites. If repairs to vehicles cannot be undertaken, children may be living in uninhabitable or potentially dangerous conditions. When repeated evictions mean that little overnight stopping is available, obtaining essential items is even more difficult (Davis, 1997, p 128).

Money

With increased eviction comes a reduced ability to stay in one area long enough to gain and retain training and employment. Repeated eviction can make festivals and gatherings more difficult to arrange or attend; Travelling People not only socialise at such events but also trade goods and services, and might thereby be deprived of another source of income (Davis et al, 1994, pp 14-16).

Travelling People have told the TLRU about having to drop out of evening classes or college courses, and being forced to relinquish good jobs; being unable to reach them any longer following an eviction cycle which forced them to ever greater distances. In the planning and human rights case of *Sally Chapman v UK*, the report of the European Commission of 25 October 1999 noted that, to avoid court action in connection with their own land, the Chapman family returned to a nomadic life. The family were then subjected to frequent eviction action by various local authorities. "The applicant's eldest daughter had started a hairdressing course at a College of Further Education and the second daughter was about to start studying at college for a Diploma in Forestry. Both of these courses had to be abandoned and the two younger children could no longer attend school" (European Commission of Human Rights, Application No 27238/95, 33 EHRR 399 [2001], *The Times*, 30 January).

Research into the economics of the 'new' Traveller communities has found that:

> Mobility was important in giving access to seasonal agricultural employment. But enforced mobility, through eviction, made regular employment very difficult to sustain ... if travellers are to gain greater access to the labour market while maintaining their travelling lifestyle, the key priorities for policy are: improving access to employment programmes and making these sensitive to the particular needs of travellers; more flexible benefits which can support temporary and seasonal employment; and – very importantly – access to stable and secure sites. (Webster and Millar, 2001, p 1)

The earlier reference to increased diesel fuel costs by the young Scottish Traveller is not the only suggestion of real financial costs to Travelling People brought to the attention of the TLRU. For example, one Traveller parent told the Unit that when her family was being moved on, "we have to take the kids out for dinner as we cannot cook. Or buy things at service stations. It's much more expensive". Another has said, "You wouldn't believe it but we still even got evicted during that fuel crisis in 2000. You'd think the police would have more to worry about. And we were running really low on diesel too". Other Travelling People have pointed out that, as taxpayers, unauthorised encampments cost them money through taxes.

Public services

Costs related to service provision may fall on providers as well as those with service-related needs. Teachers may waste hours driving around looking for an unauthorised encampment that they have been told exists, but which has been moved on by another person employed by their authority in a different capacity. In addition to the consequent damage to relationships between different employees and departments of the same authority, there is also breakdown of those between Travelling People and their service providers. Relationships of trust are difficult to establish and maintain in these circumstances.

———

Travelling People have reported feeling trauma, dislocation and distrust and dislike of 'authority' as a result of repeated eviction. In respect of the police, their participation in some eviction processes led one Gypsy woman to tell the TLRU that it takes away the feeling the police might in any way exist for the benefit of Travelling People; so that they might not ask for help when they need it. It can also be a barrier if police then come onto a site for friendly reasons: "How do you break the ice?"

Reports by government bodies charged with reviewing education have identified problems for Travelling People for nearly 30 years.

> Among the chief obstacles to access and regular attendance is the nomadic lifestyle of most of the families concerned. The education system is naturally designed to meet the needs of a static population. Attending many different schools for short periods can undermine educational progress, and in some cases, even the motivation to attend. For many Gypsy and New Travellers, the situation has been exacerbated by involuntary movement in consequence of evictions from unauthorised land. (OfSTED, 1996, p 20)

In one extreme case, an Irish Traveller child was deprived from attending school by evictions, and eventually deprived of his life at the age of seven, when a vehicle ran over him during an eviction. The eviction took place in a London area, on a day and at a time when he should have been in school.

The Save the Children Fund research mentioned in the case study in Chapter Three looked into how being 'moved on' affected the educational opportunities of Travellers. Education service providers told researchers that eviction could lead to a lack of consistent stable educational experiences, bound to be detrimental to any child's development (although such experiences do not necessarily have to be a part of the formal school system. The TLRU has met young children who can strip a generator or recognise every herb in the field, but such knowledge does not form part of the national curriculum).

Children who are moved on face interruption to formal learning and find it increasingly difficult to reintegrate into new schools. Being moved on creates negative experiences, negative expectations (on the part of children and service providers alike) and poor community relations. Mainstream education interrupted by eviction can establish erratic learning patterns and lead to poor perceptions of 'authority' in children (Morran et al, 1999, p 8).

In the same SCF research, health service providers were asked what impact being moved on had on the health of Travellers. The main effects were identified as being: inability to follow up treatment, "often resulting in the treatment of symptoms rather than causes", and the late detection of abnormalities and sometimes misdiagnosis; lack of continuity of care and disrupted treatment and education; reinforcement of mistrust of officials and 'the system' resulting in low self-esteem and confidence levels; and a reluctance to take preventative healthcare, particularly 'well woman' and immunisation services (Morran et al, 1999, p 9).

A research report focusing on social services provision for Travelling People expressed concern about the problems created by a lack of sites, resulting eviction from unauthorised encampments, and the push into housing. The report also found that services to Travelling People suffered where mobility was high due to the fixed, bureaucratic, referral-based and sometimes long-term nature of social service systems.

> These pressures create considerable challenges for social services, precisely because it is these kinds of interactions which can put social services in the role of promoting assimilation of Gypsies and Travellers and undermining their culture. This is exacerbated in situations where social services do not have a solid groundwork of understanding and familiarity with Traveller communities and culture. Without this groundwork social services' interaction with such families runs a grave risk of further isolating and pathologising them, rather than assisting them to strengthen their community connections. (Cemlyn, 1998, p 89)

As was outlined in Chapter Two, as a result of lack and loss of pitches on lawful sites, and life 'on the road' becoming untenable, many Travelling People are being pushed or pulled into housing. This can have a variety of negative follow-on effects:

> [M]any younger Travellers in housing estates face a crisis, because they are sometimes not accepted as Travellers by other Travellers, and they are not accepted by settled people as their neighbours. The negative images of Travellers affect their confidence and their pride in their own identity and community and their desire to protect or change it. (Joyce, 1999, p 37)

One Traveller, who cares for several disabled members of the family, told the TLRU of having to move into housing as eviction made proper family care difficult and access to care assistance impossible. "Disabled Travellers get such a raw deal; their problems are just trebled if they try to keep Travelling. Living in the house is easier in some ways but we're really unhappy and I'm desperate to get out." Research on social services provision has found that delays in the referral process and the impact of a nomadic way of life "meant that families had moved on before a service was provided or an appropriate carer found" (Webb, 1999).

Most goods and services that, subject to income, most settled people take for granted are designed to function in relation to a sedentary existence. Travelling People can therefore experience difficulties in areas such as obtaining insurance for living and working vehicles, legal advice, welfare benefits, voting rights; accumulating adequate paperwork to get a bank account, a mortgage, a loan, a right to participate in 'local' schemes; and organising collectively in order to access such social programmes as neighbourhood renewal funding and Sure Start.

Much has been said thus far about the existence, numbers and scale of unauthorised encampments, related costs, and how resented such sites can be.

It should also be said that Travelling People themselves often resent them too. Those living on unauthorised sites,

> ... have no access to ordinary washing or toilet facilities, although most local authorities try to make provision for the disposal of rubbish. These encampments, however, tend to be of a poor environmental standard, especially if the site is occupied for a long period. Living in such poor conditions must have a detrimental effect on Traveller health, especially among the children and teenage population, but there is little evidence available. (Advisory Committee on Scotland's Travelling People, 1998, p 21)

Social costs

In addition to the harm that can be effected on relationships between Travelling and non-Travelling communities (see Appendix E for an example of attitudes towards Travellers in Northern Ireland), and the long-term costs of deprivation and social exclusion, environmental damage has also been identified as being associated with unauthorised encampments. The Chartered Institute of Environmental Health (CIEH) has stated that:

> Besides being an attack on the lifestyle of a minority group, the Criminal Justice Act has created a 'merry-go-round' of evictions, moving the travelling communities from one local authority to another. This has been financially wasteful and environmentally damaging ... the potential health risks, both to the public and the travellers, of inadequate sites include water-borne disease through inadequate water supply and food-borne disease through unclean or overcrowded conditions. Other risks include infestation by body lice because of overcrowded conditions, refuse accumulation, accidents, fire and risks associated with living on contaminated land. (Press release, 1 July 1998, CPR98027)

The impact of environmental damage associated with unauthorised encampments is likely to be very small in the overall context of environmental problems in the UK, but the problems identified by the CIEH are nonetheless valid.

Evictions can damage relationships within and between Travelling communities. One person explained to the TLRU how an established site can be unintentionally damaged by the arrival nearby of Travelling People evicted from elsewhere. "The Travellers on the local site are seen to be from the same 'group' (even if they don't know each other), because they're Travellers too, the permanent site gets dragged into it and seen as a problem because the camp is. This is even when they've been on the proper sites for ages".

'Tolerated' unauthorised encampments can also be affected by the arrival of others evicted from another site; police or local authorities may not continue to 'tolerate' a site once it expands and all those on it, including the original occupants, may be evicted yet again. A 'new' Traveller in Somerset told the

TLRU how he had closed a gate on the (unauthorised) site where he lived with a few others – there was a photographer, an actress, a musician and an electrician on site – to prevent others coming on, even though he felt bad about it, because he knew that if he allowed them on, they would then all be forced off anyway.

Of course, relationships between Travelling and settled communities are also made more difficult by the process of enforced nomadism, and by the closure of lawful or suitable sites which forces Travelling People onto ever more visible and less suitable pieces of land (including playing fields and car parks). This relationship is not generally improved by the often markedly inflammatory and lopsided treatment of encampment issues by local press (Morris, 2000), and the common presence of police services. As one Gypsy man has put it, the media "think we're scum because they only ever see us in trouble. We see the police more than anyone in the whole country I think, all because we've nowhere to stop".

It is not only settled local people who can grow to despise or fear Travelling People, regardless of what they might be like as individuals. Some public servants too, charged with the task of perpetually moving them on, develop contempt for entire communities: "I don't care if your whole family is in hospital, I want you out of the county"[1]. This lack of respect and empathy from other people, including those in authority, has clear ramifications not only for Travelling People, but for the fair and effective delivery of public services and for the cohesion of society as a whole.

Political leaders often speak of the importance of fostering a diverse society, where difference is not only respected but valued, leading to a more vibrant and cohesive national community. The UK is, however, in danger of losing ancient and important cultures through a deliberate process of assimilation. "There are no new memories being made now we're stuck in houses because there's no bits left to stop on. They're all Tescos and ASDAs now", says one young Irish Traveller woman.

The dominance of 'majoritarian' culture harms not only non-majoritarian groups but also, ultimately, society as a whole is poorer for it. Eviction stops the education of settled society; that is, it promotes not only a lack of contact but places a wedge between communities, creating a cycle of poor social relations and understanding. "You must have done something wrong to be evicted; that's how we're always seen", says one Gypsy man. Settled and Travelling communities, when they do get together, can learn a lot from each other.

On 10 April 2002, Philip Willan reported in *The Guardian* that an Italian Gypsy, Santino Spinelli, who survived as a child by begging on the streets, would become the first Rom to hold a university post teaching a (mandatory) course in his own culture when he began teaching on Gypsy language and culture at Trieste University the following day. Mr Spinelli was quoted as saying that:

> Prejudice exists where there is a lack of knowledge. Social aspects become
> confused with a cultural model, and the error of individuals leads to the

condemnation of an entire community ... the European public has been deprived of its right to know. Romany culture belongs to humanity.... It is important that we meet one another and be enriched by our diversity.

There are some settled people, even in positions of political power, who are well aware of the deep divisions engendered by inequality, and who sometimes get the opportunity to try to effect a positive and constructive change. Lord Avebury, who has seen the tide of his efforts rise and ebb again in the guise of the 1968 Caravan Sites Act, has said that:

> If the travelling people are left to deal with this problem on their own, we shall be storing up trouble for the future, as their children grow up uneducated or semi-literate, unemployable, suffering bad health, and prey to appalling social problems. Even if we are not concerned with the human waste and suffering this implies, the cost of picking up the pieces will be far greater than the bill for completing the unfinished business of 1968 today. (Morris and Clements, 1999, p xix)

At Appleby Fair a TLRU researcher asked a Gypsy man what evictions and unauthorised encampments generally cost him and his young family. He simply replied "Dignity. It costs us our dignity".

There are, of course, major difficulties in quantifying these human 'costs', but they are nonetheless real, in terms of deprivation, a cycle of exclusion and low esteem, in terms of human pride and dignity, and in terms of the potential loss of cultural identity and way of life. Additionally, it is clear that while children are strongly affected by the experience of eviction, their voices are rarely heard throughout the process. The problems associated with quantifying these costs does not mean that they do not exist, or do not 'count'. These voices too must be heard, and not simply for emotive reasons. As part of research work tied to a professional code of ethics (including assured confidentiality for local authority respondents) and an academic standard, all of the costs associated with unauthorised encampments must be located and included.

> So Gypsies who have maintained their traditional itinerant lifestyle are faced with the following dilemma. They can either opt for stability and integration into the sedentary world in order to qualify for social assistance, rent relief, proper schooling, and so on, but at the price of giving up their mobility and, with it, many of the available opportunities for earning a living; or they can maintain their old way of life at the price of losing their social, and often political rights (voting, participating in public life), because they are largely incompatible with such mobility. (Council of Europe, 1995, p 11)

The police service

In August 2000, Thames Valley Police undertook a one-day operation in which nearly 500 Travelling People were evicted from six unauthorised encampment locations. Many of those so encamped were escorted along the motorway to the county (Berkshire) boundary ('When humans behave like animals', *The Independent*, 25 August 2000)[2]. The action by this police force would have resulted in neighbouring forces and authorities incurring expenses and using resources to deal with the resultant 'extra' unauthorised encampments in their areas. The cost of this action to the Thames Valley force itself must also have been considerable.

This incident is only one, albeit sizeable, example of police action that takes place in the UK almost daily. Despite the lack of cohesive data, it has been shown that some debate around reform of the 1968 Caravan Sites Act indicated police resources in this context to be a matter of some concern. Subsequent secondary sources indicate that these concerns are ongoing. For example:

> [W]ithout an area to direct trespassers to go, all the police can do is to remove the trespassers from one piece of land with the inevitable consequence that they will go elsewhere, provoking more expense, resources and associated issues. That is why the Police and Local Authority have recognised that in order to avoid continually spending ratepayers' money recycling the problem around the town, it would be better value to work towards finding a site to which Travellers can be directed. (Northamptonshire Police, 2000)

The excerpt comes from *Travellers in Northamptonshire*, an information document on unauthorised encampments produced by Northamptonshire Police (issued in 2000). The Traveller Policy Officer within that force sits on the Northamptonshire County Council Best Value Review Group on Unauthorised Encampments, set up in 2000. (Gloucestershire County Council commenced a Best Value Review of Traveller Services in 2002; it appears that now at least a few local authorities are beginning to think of encampments and related issues in this context, and interestingly it appears to be authorities that are already engaged in some form of interagency working.)

The costs to the police would include the collection, storing, retrieval, sharing, analysis and updating of information held on police computer systems about Travelling People and their vehicles and movements. For example, the draft Police Notice detailing changes to the Metropolitan Police Service policy on unauthorised camping and the use of 1994 CJPOA police powers states that, in areas where 'incursions' regularly take place, a Gypsy or Traveller Liaison Officer should be appointed as a part-time post holder within existing Crime and Disorder partnership structures. The officer's duties would include extensive information-related activities (MPS Public Order Policy Unit, 2000).

Substantial resources will be expanded in those areas where the police are inclined to become involved in unauthorised encampments that do not represent a substantial threat to public order; those that do present such a threat being fairly infrequent, according to government-commissioned research (see Chapter One on the nature of unauthorised encampments).

In the recent study undertaken for the DETR/DTLR by Cowan et al (2001), 22 (73%) of the 30 responding police forces had some local authorities in their area with a written Gypsy and Traveller strategy or protocol, including two force areas with no recent experience of unauthorised encampments. In eight cases all the local authorities in the police force area had such documents. In all 22 areas the police forces had been consulted in the development of such a strategy. More than two thirds of respondents (19) said that the police had a written protocol with the local authorities in their area regarding the best practice approach to encampments, with the local authority taking the lead role in most areas (pp 40-1).

However, as was also found in 1998 through Home Office research (Bucke and James, 1998; see Chapter Two), in some areas the police seem reluctant to become involved with unauthorised encampments. In these areas the police do not view their role as being appropriate to the activities concerned with unauthorised encampments, where an 'enforcement' role may be complicated by (or conflict with) extensive social welfare considerations; or come close to being a special protection agency for private landowners. "The proposed criminal sanctions which could result in the impounding of their homes are unacceptable. These sanctions are unlikely to be attractive to police forces because acting as enforcement bailiffs in such matters is not what police officers think of as 'proper policing duties'" (*Police Review*, 28 August 1992).

Of course, such reluctance may be seen by other parties as a contributor to the causes and costs to them of having to deal with unauthorised encampments. In its response to the 1992 consultation paper on reform of the Caravan Sites Act (see Chapter Two), Slough Estates PLC asserted: "The knowledge that the police do not wish to become involved is a significant contributory cause of the increase in invasions".

Other landowners

In a letter from a resident of Mitcham, Surrey, to the editor of *The Surrey Guardian* it was said that "[A quoted police officer] may think clear-up costs are exaggerated but he has not, like me, written to landowners to find out the facts. The sums really are large, usually between £10,000 and £20,000 per site" (16 November 2000). In the same year, a senior surveyor at the firm Rogers Chapman was quoted in *Estates Gazette* as saying:

> To remove travellers from an industrial estate in Greenford, our client had to pay legal fees for a court order to be served as well as pay for a personal appearance by a court official to serve the order. Clear-up costs for the site have been estimated at anything from £3,000-£6,000 to remove fly-tipping, general household rubbish, nappies and so on. The quicker you remove the squatters, the less it costs. (24 June 2000, p 63)

While the TLRU survey was not specifically directed at identifying the costs for private landowners affected by unauthorised encampments, archival information from secondary sources suggests that these can be substantial. By way of example, a letter read to the House of Commons during a debate on 'Travellers' in 1999 stated:

> As I look out of the window of our factory ... I can count 42 caravans, 6 horses and dogs too numerous to count. Caravans and vehicles are parked within feet of the factory, the reception area is being used as a human toilet and we cannot open any windows because of the awful smell. Customers and suppliers are refusing to visit the factory. This is creating severe difficulties, not to mention loss of business and the subsequent loss of jobs – we are grinding to a halt. (House of Commons Hansard Debates, 19 July 1999, col 941)

Further such evidence has been provided by the Northamptonshire Chamber of Commerce, which carried out a survey of its membership on Travellers' encampments, and reported the findings in August 1998. Of the 171 members that responded to a questionnaire, 96 were aware of encampments within the vicinity of their premises within the previous 12 months. Fifty-one respondents had taken preventative measures such as building soil bunds, ditches or barriers to discourage Travellers from returning to their property. The cost of undertaking these measures ranged from £50 to £27,000, with an average cost of £5,390 per respondent. Sixty-four respondents felt that their business had been directly affected by unauthorised encampments, and problems referred to included damage to premises and vehicles, theft, dumping of rubbish, parking problems, noise disturbance, and customer and staff harassment.

Most respondents who had been directly affected by the encampments had contacted the local authority (53) and the police (56) for assistance. Twenty-four had contacted a solicitor and ten had contacted other organisations such as the Chamber of Commerce, their landlord, MP or the county council. Twenty-three were satisfied with the assistance provided and 39 were not. A common response was that action by the police and/or councils was too slow, and many referred to a lack of interest. It was the view of some that authorities were unable to take action due to "lack of power".

In addition to surveying local authorities as part of the TLRU research, the Unit wrote to the Crown Estate Commissioners, the Duchy of Lancaster, English Nature, Forest Enterprise, the Ministry of Agriculture Fisheries & Food, and the Ministry of Defence to request information about expenditure related to unauthorised encampments. Of the six central government departments listed, two responded to the questionnaire.

One department was unable to account for staff time spent dealing with two cases against unauthorised encampments (obtaining possession orders against Travellers illegally occupying "specially designated and sensitive" land), but were able to give exact figures for the legal costs of these actions (£8,232.58).

The other department gave an approximate figure of £51,800; £46,800 in respect of legal costs and the remaining £5,000 for attributable staff costs.

This small and partial accounting alone adds £60,000 to the UK total for one year. It is unknown how much other public landowners expend, and impossible to know how much private landowners spend, on the costs of seeking possession orders, land protection, clean-up costs and so on. Just the sparse evidence noted here suggests that the total annual sum is likely to be in the millions of pounds.

The planning system

As already noted, few respondents to the TLRU survey identified costs associated with the planning aspects of unauthorised encampments; that is, encampments on land in the ownership of Travelling People, which does not have planning permission for such use. It could well be that this type of unauthorised encampment is seen differently from encampments on land in the ownership of people other than those encamped upon it. Nonetheless, separate research and other evidence indicates that the planning system both incurs and creates significant costs in respect of such encampments.

Accompanying the 1994 legislative changes, amendments were made to planning guidance. This rescinded the 'privileged position' that Gypsies were alleged to have in respect of gaining permission to reside on green belt land in their ownership under earlier guidance (DoE, 1977). The justification for the new Circular 1/94 (DoE and Welsh Office, 1994b) was that it put Gypsy applicants for planning permission on an 'equal footing' with other 'developers', although local planning authorities were also counselled to include a policy on Gypsy sites in local plans.

The Advisory Council for the Education of Romany and other Travellers (ACERT) has undertaken research into Gypsies and the planning system, finding that needless expense is incurred by applicants, local authorities and the Planning Inspectorate, especially as many cases go to appeal unnecessarily. Identifying 'clear difficulties' for applicants, ACERT suggests that:

> ... it is no wonder the majority of applications are retrospective [made after the land is purchased]. For many Gypsies this route offers the only alternative to camping on the roadside. By buying and occupying their own land and applying for permission – even if refused – an appeal can offer valuable time and a chance of success. This method of provision is haphazard, costly and lengthy for both applicant and authority. (Williams, 1999, p xii)

The *Directory of planning policies for Gypsy site provision in England* (ACERT and Wilson, 1997) gathered together in one document all existing policies on Gypsy sites. This enabled an assessment of which authorities had policies, what kind of policies there were, what kind of criteria were being used in criteria-based policies, and what effect Circular 1/94 was having on encouraging the adoption of Gypsy site policies in development plans.

The research found that almost one third of local authorities still had no policy on Gypsy site provision in their development plans. Of those authorities that had formulated a policy, by far the most common type was the criteria-based policy: 63 different criteria being in use in England, between two and 12 per policy. (This is a policy in which, rather than a specific location or locations being identified as appropriate for sites, a number of criteria are listed which an applicant could or should meet in respect of the land on which they wish to reside.) Thirty-five percent of criteria-based policies stated that planning permission would be granted where the criteria were met; the remainder stated that permission might be granted in that circumstance or that the authority would take account of the criteria. While Circular 1/94 had required that policies should identify locations for sites where appropriate, only two English local authorities (of 403) had actually allocated land for a specific site in their plan.

The research also found that the criteria used varied considerably between different authorities, but that most of them related to location, potential impact or site design. Sixty-three percent of authorities imposed a criterion that sites should have no impact or minimal impact on amenities of local residents or adjoining land uses. Forty-one percent stipulated that sites should not be located in 'protected areas', such as green belt, Sites of Special Scientific Interest (SSSIs), Areas of Outstanding Natural Beauty (AONBs), Conservation Areas or other 'designated areas of restraint'. Criteria requiring that sites should have no impact or minimal impact on the environment or character and appearance of the countryside were adopted by 41% of authorities.

ACERT concluded that "many local authorities seem to be going against the intentions of Circular 1/94 either by ignoring its advice and producing no policy, or seizing on parts of it which appear to support their own restrictive policy on Gypsy sites" (ACERT and Wilson, 1997, p 10). The DETR-commissioned research into the use of powers for managing unauthorised camping (Niner et al, 1998) referred to in Chapter One, found that in the background to the problem of large unauthorised encampments were wider questions of planning policies and site provision. The report suggested that criteria-based policies in local plans made such provision extremely difficult, especially in areas of planning restraint. Some local authority areas consist of little more than areas of housing and restricted areas zoned as 'green belt' or other protective zonal classifications.

In 1999 ACERT published a further report, *Private Gypsy site provision* (Williams, 1999). It found that Circular 1/94 has not helped to achieve greater certainty. Gypsy site policies provide little locational certainty, and most local authorities do not know where to expect private Gypsy site development locations. The identification of potential Gypsy site locations within development plans had still not been taken up by local authorities. The criteria-based policies preferred by authorities had provided little certainty for applicants when deciding where best to locate new Gypsy sites, and thereby limited the capability of plan-led provision. Five years on from the introduction of Circular

1/94, the increase in private site provision had not even offset the decrease in public site provision:

> At the current rate it will take 10 years for caravans on unauthorised sites to decrease to zero. During the same time if the pace of private and public site provision does not increase, provision will not be made for new families wishing to live on authorised caravan sites. This sector of the Gypsy population will largely live either in caravans on unauthorised sites or move into housing.... If these trends continue, the extent to which the ethnic, cultural and linguistic identity of Gypsy and Traveller people will be protected and promoted is questionable. (Williams, 1999, p vii)

The ACERT research suggests that many planning applications by Travelling People have to go to appeal. Their study examined 624 Gypsy site appeals and found that 63% were dismissed and 28% allowed. Of all planning authorities, 43% were involved in Gypsy site appeals between 1988 and 1998, showing a national demand for private sites (pp viii–ix).

Enforcement and appeal proceedings are costly for authorities; paid assistance for applicants and appellants, in the form of lawyers and/or planning consultants, can mount up, in addition to fees, stress, uncertainty, and the cost of land that cannot be lived on if application and appeal are unsuccessful. The relationship between unauthorised encampments and the planning system is an example of how the costs of encampments generally can be complex and widespread, both in their causes and effects.

One example of how significant the costs in this arena can be is provided by Mid Bedfordshire District Council, which determined to evict Travelling People from their own land (Woodside Caravan Park) for which no planning permission had been granted. According to the Council, the estimated revenue cost of the action proposed (including eviction of persons, removal of buildings and other site clearance action, and legal costs) was £180,000. No budget existed for this expenditure and the Executive of the Council were asked to approve supplementary revenue (20 June 2001)[3]. The Travelling People concerned expressed to the TLRU (by e-mail) their concerns as to the costs to themselves in the course of this action: stress, family fragmentation, time, legal costs, and the fear of homelessness and loss of property. Money well spent?

Notes

[1] Police officer to a Traveller woman during eviction from an unauthorised site, after she told him that her six-month-old baby was in hospital with pneumonia. From the newsletter of the Traveller Advice Team, the Community Law Partnership, Birmingham, February 1999.

[2] Since this operation took place, Thames Valley Police have written a force-wide policy on unauthorised encampments (December 2000), in which it is acknowledged that all action taken in respect of encampments has the potential to engage Articles 5, 8 and 11

of the European Convention on Human Rights; and that all such action should therefore be necessary, safe, lawful, proportionate and balanced.

[3] The Executive Committee Papers of this District Council are available at www.midbeds.gov.uk

FIVE

Best Value

'Best Value' has been defined as "securing continuous improvement in the exercise of all functions undertaken by [an] authority, whether statutory or not, having regard to a combination of economy, efficiency and effectiveness" (DETR, 1999, paragraph 3). The 1999 Local Government Act (LGA) imposes on most bodies within the local government finance system in Britain, including police and fire services, a duty to make arrangements for the achievement of Best Value in the performance of their functions.

The duty came into force from 1 April 2000, accompanying mandatory duties to consult with representative groups of specific categories of people, and to refer to any relevant guidance issued by the Secretary of State. Section 5 of the 1999 LGA states that Best Value authorities must review all of their functions within a time period specified by the Secretary of State (initially, probably, a period of five years). Local performance plans relating to Best Value must then:

- Provide local people with a summary of how far the authority was successful in meeting the objectives and performance targets of the previous year, and the results of its performance as compared with that of other Best Value authorities.
- Inform local people of the performance targets it has set itself for the following year and future years, where necessary, and the extent to which it is on the way to meeting any longer-term targets. Where it is not on course, this may include an outline of what action(s) it is taking to remedy the situation.
- Summarise the outcome of the reviews carried out under section 5, which will usually be expressed in the form of revised targets, and the future programme for achieving them.

The Audit Commission has powers of inspection under section 10 of the LGA to assess compliance with the requirements of Best Value, and retains duties under the 1998 Audit Commission Act to set local authority 'performance indicators'.

The principles of Best Value include that the duty is owed by local authorities to local people, both as taxpayers and customers of local authority services. Performance plans should support the process of local accountability to the electorate. Achieving Best Value is not just about economy and efficiency, but also effectiveness and the quality of local services – so that the setting of targets and performance against these should underpin the regime. The true key to Best Value is striking a balance between cost and quality.

The duty should be applied to a wider range of services than those covered under the former regime of compulsory competitive tendering (CCT). Details are to be developed between local authority departments, the Audit Commission and the Local Government Association. Central government continues to set the basic framework for service provision, which includes national standards[1].

A stated aim of the new regime is to:

> ... set a demanding new performance framework for local [and police] authorities. It will challenge them to re-assess their aims and objectives, the nature of local needs, the capacity of local government (and its partners) to meet these needs, and the resources available in the short and long term. Above all, Best Value will emphasise that the ultimate responsibility of local authorities is to the local people who pay for and use the services and facilities that they provide. (Audit Commission, 1998, p 5)

The government's Best Value pilot programme involved 45 authorities in 41 pilots, including county, metropolitan and London borough councils, shire unitary authorities, shire districts, Welsh unitary authorities, and fire and police services. Pilots were selected in late 1997 and the pilot programme commenced in April 1998.

Since the pilot programme was completed, local authorities have been provided with a great deal of guidance as to the broad approaches they might want to take, the structures they may wish to build and the general aims they should work to in meeting the LGA duty. However, authorities retain a great deal of discretion and have been left to work out the particulars appropriate to the needs of their areas.

The duty is not of Best Value per se but of 'continuous improvement' in those areas previously outlined, through the medium of authorities' corporate policies and objectives. Enshrined in the Best Value legislation are what have become known as the 'four Cs'.

- Challenge: of the four, potentially the most revolutionary. Local authorities are to become community leaders, challenging pre-existing and preconceived ways of working. This is to be undertaken in the context of increasingly restrictive budgets, although new ideas and changes need not necessarily be expensive.
- Compare: rather than simple fact checking and figure comparison, the guidance suggests that it may be more useful to ask 'how are things done elsewhere?'. This exercise can prove valuable, provided that the ultimate purpose of Best Value is borne in mind.
- Consult: this serves a wider 'democratic renewal' agenda, implying that authorities have not in the past been sufficiently engaged with the people that they serve. Authorities are advised to ensure that consultation reaches out – 'one size fits all' techniques are unlikely to work – and that consultation can take place with a wide range of parties including community groups, non-governmental organisations, churches and local business groups.

- Compete: the guidance suggests that this principle provides an opportunity to move forward, from definitions and packages under the previous CCT programme, to more rigorous examination of alternative approaches and varied solutions.

Although there is not formally a fifth 'C', collaboration is often included as one; that is, working in partnership with other bodies, public and private, to ensure Best Value. There can, of course, sometimes be a fine line between collaboration and collusion, which should be guarded against.

The Audit Commission and Best Value pilot programme publications identify key issues of Best Value implementation for any authority to include involving elected members, at least insofar as they are 'signed up' to Best Value. The full council must adopt a Best Value Performance Plan (BVPP); ensure that the authority has clear policies and objectives; must manage expectations and keep in touch with reality (particularly during wide consultation); learn and 'capacity build' (especially important for smaller and/or more tightly-run authorities); demonstrating that the authority has come to reasonable conclusions based on reasonable evidence. The government maintains the importance of garnering clear evidence of the impact of changes. All authorities are not, of course, obliged to reach the same conclusions; there should be a balance between mimicry and innovation.

Other outcomes include that, while the government has always added the proviso of 'within the resources available', many authorities say the process works better when dedicated resources are applied and therefore when funding mechanisms for Best Value achievement are formalised. Good conduct remains essential; the Nolan Committee on Standards in Public Life (1996) identified seven important principles of public life that should be adhered to: selflessness, integrity, objectivity, accountability, openness, honesty and leadership by example.

Probably the most major change brought about by the Best Value programme in practice is the imposition of a comprehensive inspection regime. According to the Audit Commission inspection fact sheet[2], questions that will be asked by the Commission as part of inspections include:

- how good are the services that have been inspected? Possible ratings run from 3 stars = excellent to 0 stars = poor;
- will they improve in the way that Best Value requires? Auditors can conclude 'yes', 'probably' or 'unlikely';
- does a service meet its aims?;
- how does its performance compare?;
- does the Best Value review drive improvement?;
- how good is the improvement plan?;
- will the authority deliver the improvements?;
- are the authority's aims clear and challenging?

Best Value and consultation

As there has been no duty on local authorities in England and Wales to provide Gypsy sites since November 1994, there is concurrently no explicit requirement to measure Best Value in relation to unauthorised encampments. Nonetheless, the performance of acts and omissions under various statutes and local policies by public authorities in relation to unauthorised encampments would fall within the definition of Best Value and its aims. Only one of the respondents to the TLRU research on the costs of unauthorised encampments expressly mentioned Best Value in relation to them.

An important aspect of the Best Value initiative is that the ultimate responsibility of local authorities is to 'local' people, who pay for and use the services and facilities that they provide. That Travelling People on unauthorised encampments tend not to be seen as 'local' is clear from the response to the relevant question in the TLRU costs survey (see Chapter Three as to 'local' and 'long distance'). One respondent stressed: "*All* travellers are regarded as long-distance". Therefore, Travelling People might not be seen as relevant to the measurement and assessment of service functions. (Although those permanently resident on local sites may be in a different position, this should not be assumed.)

Best Value may in one sense be considered as a potential tool for 'social inclusion'. It is a means of ensuring that people are included in the decision-making processes and subsequent actions that affect their lives. The TLRU costs research suggests that local authorities essentially opt for one of three approaches to unauthorised encampments in this context:

1) A 'neutral' approach, in which Travelling People are seen neither as entitled to nor part of a value for money programme. They are simply not noticed unless and until they become seen as a 'problem' (at which point the 'negative' approach might be more likely to be taken).
2) A 'negative' approach, which lays stress on the 'local', that is local people, local taxpayers, the local electorate. This is a positive and lucid value, but implicitly sanctions negative action against perceived 'non-locals'. The TLRU research suggests that in some authorities this approach has resulted or will result in exclusion; that, whether by act or omission, Travelling People suffer, since they are more likely than not to be seen as belonging 'elsewhere'.
3) A 'positive' approach, whereby all people with whom local authority service providers engage are automatically assumed to be 'local', and to fall within local initiatives of Best Value and other authority policies and programmes. An example of this approach can be found in the case study discussed later.

Responses to the TLRU costs survey indicate that some authorities consider taking a non-toleration stance to be a Best Value approach to unauthorised encampments. One city council stated that this was "not an area where cost saving is likely to be a priority. The public ... as reflected by the views of the elected members and the response to the Crime and Disorder Act surveys simply do not want travellers [here] ... the community has enough problems with its resident underclass". In other words, 'zero tolerance' is Best Value because that is what 'local people' want.

One London Borough, after considering various approaches, opted to adopt a 'zero toleration policy', noting that liaison and joint working with police to that end was henceforth evolving. (The authority's estimate of costs in the period, £73,800, was exclusive of any health, social, education or other services.) The authority stated that: "In the eyes of the public the success of the Council is measured in preventing Traveller encampments, the speed of eviction and the speed of returning the land to its normal use".

In such cases it is clear that Travelling People are not seen as part of 'the public' and therefore Best Value considerations do not apply to them in the same manner as to other people living locally. The challenges posed by unauthorised encampments evidently raise serious questions concerning the intellectual rigor of aspects of the Best Value approach. For whose benefit does Best Value exist? To which persons in an area does the need for Best Value apply?

As already noted, local authorities must demonstrate that they have carried out relevant consultation during each fundamental service review, rather than simply consulting people as users or potential users of services. They are therefore primarily engaging with people as taxpayers, and so must also involve local businesses and other agencies that have an interest about the area as a whole, and about the council's mission and priorities.

The Audit Commission specifically suggests that topics on which authorities might seek to engage with local people include: what they want for the area and their community; the authority's overall values and priorities; how these affect specific decisions; the balance between spending and local taxes in annual budgeting; views of how well the council does its job and how it could improve; the overall local performance plan; the authority's approach in carrying out its role as advocate for the local area; and any controversial individual decisions that the authority might make (Audit Commission, 1998, p 40).

In this context, Travelling People might more often be seen as the subject of consultation rather than potential consultees. The justification for the exclusion stems not merely from the perception that Travelling People are 'non-local', but also from the not uncommon belief that Travelling People do not pay council taxes. Whereas, since the majority (perhaps two thirds or more) of Travelling People are settled on permanent sites or in houses, they have the same relationship to the local tax system as all people living in conventional housing.

Where Travelling People *are* seen as group with whom it is proper to consult, undertaking consultation and achieving a meaningful dialogue with the Travelling communities may not always be a simple matter. After all, effective consultation must be more than a tokenistic exercise.

> Effective consultation is particularly difficult and challenging when communities such as Gypsies are involved. Their historic and daily interaction with officialdom is invariably troubled. Officials are rarely carriers of good

news. It is not surprising that they may not seek out such contact but we should also accept that their reluctance to participate is not based on indifference but previous experience. (Thomas and Campbell, 1992, p 1)

Indeed, the Audit Commission has identified 'Travellers' as a 'hard to reach' group in the context of consultation, as have the Office for National Statistics in relation to the inclusion of Travelling People in the 2001 National Census. Some police research has also included Travelling People in studies of 'hard to reach' groups, albeit in a somewhat perfunctory and adversary-focused manner:

> As a key local service, police authorities and their respective forces are required to respond to the Best Value initiative, not least by reviewing and improving consultation mechanisms ... it is well-established that some social groups are more likely than others to come into adversarial contact with the police ... problematic relationships arising not primarily from economic deprivation, but rather from factors connected with lifestyle and culture. For example, discussions have focused upon relations between the police and young people in general (Loader, 1996), lesbians and gay men (Derbyshire, 1990; Burke, 1994) and gypsy and traveller groups ... although universal popular approval for the police can never be a realistic aim of police–community relations policies, improved dialogue with marginalised groups may provide the opportunities for addressing aspects of policing that exacerbate adversarial relationships. At a minimum, it should enhance the possibility of achieving some workable compromises. (Jones and Newburn, 2001, pp 20-1)

Despite potential difficulties, the Best Value guidance requires that local authorities and police attempt to tackle obstacles such as those identified here. That something might be difficult or different is not sufficient justification for an authority not to attempt it. According to the Audit Commission:

> Overcoming barriers to consultation is just one aspect of ensuring that all sections of the community benefit from the improvements that it is hoped will flow from Best Value. Equal opportunities considerations should feature at both a corporate and service-specific level when implementing Best Value. A failure to scrutinise equality of access during fundamental performance review may lead to higher costs (through, for example, higher than necessary risk of litigation) and lower quality of service for those users who continue to receive a substandard service (or no service at all). (Audit Commission, 1998, p 70)

The role of politics

An important element in the success of Best Value is that local members are meaningfully involved in its implementation. Members are to participate in the Best Value process from the beginning, in setting clear priorities for the future; ascertaining whether their authority is performing as well as it might; committing themselves to continuous service improvement; and viewing themselves as "champions of the public's interests" (Audit Commission, 1998, p 12).

Indeed, the interim evaluation of the Best Value pilot programme found that the involvement of members had been important in:

> ... ensuring that the authority has a clear sense of corporate and service priorities; setting the overall 'tone' and strategic objectives of Best Value initiatives; overseeing the progress of Best Value reviews; supporting local communities participating in consultation associated with Best Value reviews; responding to the findings of reviews; and providing feedback to communities about the decisions that have been reached. (Martin et al, 1999, p 9)

As demonstrated in previous chapters, it is the view of some authorities that the 'public interest' is undermined by the presence of Travelling People; that Travelling People are not part of 'the public' and should be treated in a more tightly controlled fashion. One respondent to the 1992 consultation paper on reform of the Caravan Sites Act, a local councillor, stated that "Gypsies have private sites in our area and have traveled [sic] through the district to Appleby Fair for generations, the overnight stopping places are well known to gypsies and have caused no problems". However, she went on to say that:

> ... the threat of being put into a 'camp' for a fixed period of time and under control like open prisons may make the 'traveller' become more responsible for his/her own way of life ... [Gypsies could] carry a form of identity card produced by the Gypsy Council, enabling them to travel 'with permission' to their fairs in Summer.

The political dilemmas posed by unauthorised encampments are, of course, very real. Given that local authorities have little or no control over regional or national arrangements, it is not surprising that they experience difficulties in striking a balance between the rights and interests of Travelling and non-Travelling communities, or might see Travelling People as an obstacle in the way of Best Value.

The following article illustrates this dilemma well. Written by Nina Marshall in the *Southampton Echo* (17 October 2000), it was entitled 'Travellers' blight set to be tackled'. This is a long extract, but serves to highlight many of the issues and tensions that have been addressed thus far, and some yet to be addressed.

> It is the annual blight that causes huge problems for environmental health officers and residents.... Last summer a convoy of about 40 vehicles set up camp in Park Gate, near Fareham, and it cost the county council about £500 to clear up after them. But now Fareham Borough Council has come up with a new idea to deter travellers from creating an expensive clean-up bill for which taxpayers have to fork out. The council has written to the

government asking for the power to impound vehicles until unauthorised campers pay up.

But some councillors have criticised the plan. They feel it would leave travellers homeless and unable to leave the area. Housing committee chairman Ernest Crouch said it would be better to encourage travellers to use special sites provided for them. "There is no way we could impound the vehicles – it would lead to other problems, one of them being that they would not be able to leave the site while the case was heard". Labour leader Mick Prior said any measures to impound vehicles would have to be used very carefully, as the consequences for families could be dire. He said: "I would hope that if any scheme were brought in that it would be framed in a way that would prevent people becoming homeless".

Council leader Sean Woodward admitted that the motion, approved at a full council meeting last week, did have problems but said the mess and disturbance caused by travellers was unacceptable. He said the council might consider the travellers to be voluntarily homeless and so would not have a duty to actually help them. Although councillors admit the government is unlikely to accept the plan, they think its message overrides any problems in the proposed powers. Councillor Jim Murray, who seconded the motion, said: "Travellers do not help themselves – they leave the places filthy dirty, leave rubbish behind and it costs the council a lot of money". But chief executive of St. Petroc's housing association Graham Lockley said resources for the homeless in Fareham were already stretched to the limit. "Most of the provision in the area for single people is very highly used – our night shelter is always full", he said.

This example and the case study which follows later in this chapter demonstrate that, depending on the tenor and role of local politics, Best Value in relation to unauthorised encampments can be seen variously by local government officers and members as a help, a hindrance, or an irrelevance. That consultation with Travelling communities will take place to assist in the development of local policy and service delivery is not a project that could be relied on in a great many local authority areas.

Best Value and equality

The Southampton newspaper article demonstrates just one, somewhat unexamined, approach to encampments, but one that will recur in councils throughout the UK, taking little notice of equality issues. Many local authorities have equality built into their Best Value regime, in that 'equal opportunities', 'equality of opportunity' and similar phrases may be used in council mission statements or other documents fundamental to the operation of the authority. It remains to be seen whether and in how detailed a fashion the Audit Commission will measure local authority compliance with these broad statements of purpose during Best Value audits.

Equality issues are not mentioned in the Best Value principles; and the Best Value consultation paper, the Best Value White Paper, the 1999 Local Government Act and associated guidance are all silent on the topic. 'Equality' is difficult to measure, is not always inexpensive, and the benefits of pursuing it can be intangible and long-term. "Efficiency is not an exclusive criterion to be applied in policy formation: considerations of income distribution are also important. Policies which improve efficiency may increase inequalities in income distribution.... There is often a trade-off between efficiency and considerations of equity and equality" (Mulreany, 1991, pp 30-1).

Research by both the Improvement and Development Agency (IDeA) for local government and the Employers' Organisation for Local Government (which they shorten to EO) suggests that:

> ... relatively few councils are integrating equalities issues into their Best Value programmes and that the numbers don't seem to have increased significantly since [the previous] year. Far from being mainstream, there is a real concern that equality is being sidelined. The good intentions of many councils, published in written statements, to incorporate equalities policies into their strategies and review guidelines, don't happen in practice. Too many councils fall down because effective action on equality is limited to specific services, such as leisure or caring for the elderly, and not taken on across the whole council or through all the stages of planning and design of future services. (Frances Carter, Head of Best Value at the IDeA, quoted in *The Guardian*, 30 August 2000)

One factor influencing the way in which local authorities develop and structure their Best Value programmes is the lead given to them at a national level. The Best Value regime is envisaged as one in which local authorities will set their own targets against national as well as local indicators. Given the extent to which Travelling People are invisible within almost every document and programme emanating from central government – for example, the National Census, the development of housing policy (www.housing.odpm.gov.uk) – it is perhaps unsurprising that local authorities often overlook them in the 'positive', 'citizen' sense.

Current Audit Commission indicators that most clearly demonstrate the 'efficiency or effectiveness of a service' include: the percentage of housing benefit applications processed in 14 days; percentage of council tax collected; the number of books and other items issued by libraries per head of population; and the percentage of pupils in local authority schools achieving five or more A-C grade GCSEs (Audit Commission, 1998, p 80). Few of these can be said to apply to Travelling People – for example, given their problems accessing secondary education (OfSTED, 1996, 1998, 2001) – and certainly would not be relevant to the issue of unauthorised encampments or even to the general pursuance of equal opportunities.

The selection of such indicators, coupled with the following guidance on spending priorities, raises questions about the equality credentials of the Best

Value scheme. In this respect, they can assume an oppressive countenance by requiring local authorities to prioritise the prejudices of a majority, notwithstanding that they might seriously harm the interests of an excluded minority.

The Audit Commission guidance advises: "By plotting satisfaction with services against the importance that they are given by users or the public, for example, it becomes possible to focus on those services that are rated as highly important but low in satisfaction as a priority for early action" (1998, p 51). Local authorities are advised that, when deciding which services or aspects of services to address through targets and standards, they should consider public perception, and whether complaints, consumer surveys or feedback from members reveal weak spots that need particular attention. Member priorities and concerns should be ascertained, and the services used and relied on by the largest numbers of local people identified (pp 81-2).

Information provided to the TLRU in the costs survey indicated a potential issue for local authorities in this respect. Some clearly see it as a priority to move unauthorised encampments on as soon as possible, regardless of the cost or equality considerations. One respondent stated that there "is a feeling that not to endlessly repeat the eviction proceedings will give rise to the idea that [this area] is a 'soft touch' for travellers". This is not a singular view, nor one limited to local authority staff. For example, residents of one English village paid a group of Travellers £1,000 to leave their area rather than 'tolerate' or welcome them (Davis, 1997, p 130).

Some authorities even see it as worth a considerable sum of money not to have authorised encampments in their area. As a newspaper report has noted: "Travellers using a site which has been their home for more than 20 years have been given more than £200,000 to leave ... figures drawn up by officers show that to keep a reduced site would cost almost £250,000 more than shutting it down" (*The Enfield Independent*, 1 March 2000). One person quoted in the report observed that there "is currently no requirement for the council to provide a site for travelling families' caravans, whether it be of a transitory or more permanent variety. Accordingly, there would be no difficulty caused to the move-on process of travellers should the Burnside site close". A spokesperson for the relevant council stated: "The freeing up of this land provides the council with about £1.6 million and an area on which to provide cheaper accommodation for people". It is evident that this Council would be in difficulties were an 'equality proofing' exercise to be carried out into policies and practices.

Other local authorities also see unauthorised encampments as a legal and enforcement issue, to which costs attach but which is far removed from any notion of either equality or Best Value. One respondent to the TLRU research states that the:

> Council's main cause for concern was frequent occupation of business sites
> and car parks at [an] enterprise park which has some 300-400 businesses. Since
> 1998, this has been improved by Council obtaining a 'blanket' possession order

in the High Court, jointly with all of the tenants. This is successful but we have to pay high fees to bailiff and under-Sheriff each for 12 months, to cover constant 'policing'.

The issue of equality in relation to Best Value will be explored further in the following chapter on rights and race relations.

Best Value and the police service

As already noted, it is not only local authorities to whom duties under the 1999 Local Government Act apply. Police authorities are also obliged to secure "continuous improvement in the exercise of all functions", having regard to a combination of economy, efficiency and effectiveness, including looking at how best to "achieve efficiency gains to reinvest in tackling crime and disorder ... the underlying ethos of the whole approach to tackling disorder, is that investment in assessing, minimising and managing the risk of disorder is far more cost effective than spending large sums to resolve disorder when it has broken out" (HMIC, 1999, p 4).

Her Majesty's Inspectorate of Constabulary (HMIC) has, for over a century, been charged with examining and improving the efficiency of the police service in England and Wales. Unauthorised encampments are seen by HMIC as a public order issue, and public order in turn is viewed as a Best Value issue. Therefore, it is reasonable to assume that HMIC would see unauthorised encampments as a Best Value issue.

However, there appears to be little meaningful Best Value development in this area by police services, because unauthorised encampments are not usually an issue of order or disorder, but one of the lawfulness of stopping. This is not an issue over which police services have any control in terms of 'assessing, minimising and managing the risk' under Best Value.

Evidence suggests a historical reluctance on the part of police forces to take a heavy-handed 'enforcement' approach to unauthorised encampments (although, as with the majority of Travelling People who are law abiding, there are individuals whose actions belie exceptions to this generality). A civil servant, commenting on the responses of 'landowners and country interests' to the 1992 consultation paper on reform of the CSA, noted: "All of these responses mention section 39 of the POA[3] to a greater or lesser degree, some complaining that their individual police forces seem unwilling to use it against gypsies and travellers".

In 2000 a senior Home Office civil servant expressed the opinion to the TLRU that unauthorised encampments are 'unlawful' and that unlawful behaviour should never be (seen to be) tolerated; a view that resulted in minor changes to the *Good practice guide* and Circular 18/94 to 'clarify' the intended meaning of 'tolerance'. In contrast, however, the DETR has attempted, through its guidance, to persuade local authorities to reduce the incidence of encampments by 'tolerating' them whenever possible.

While such interdepartmental conflict creates difficulties for local authorities, the implications for the police are perhaps worse. Although they do not have statutorily imposed welfare responsibilities for Travelling People (under legislation such as the Education Acts, the 1989 Children Act, and so on), their 'frontline' position inevitably brings them into contact with unauthorised encampments. The absence of consistent guidance can make it difficult for them to balance their community and race relations and law enforcement roles.

HMIC states that the "cultural changes required to move a force from 'incident response' to 'problem solving' policing are considerable. However, Her Majesty's Inspector firmly believes that the long term benefits to a force and its community are considerable and fully justify the effort involved" (HMIC, 1999, p 4).

Regardless of this command to forces by HMIC to take a dynamic approach, it is a challenge for officers to take it with respect to unauthorised encampments. Under current law and policy, the only proactive role officers can employ is intelligence gathering, enabling them to move unauthorised encampments on almost before they happen. As has been considered previously, this simply shifts a 'problem' within and between force areas, neither reducing the use of resources nor representing 'problem solving policing' in the longer term. "Let us turn them off again and again and if it costs us money to do so, it is money well spent to get rid of these people" (a police officer quoted in Lambert, 1976, p 189).

Even should the police want and are able to approach unauthorised encampments as a Best Value issue, data collection and recording are likely to be difficult.

> It has not been possible to extract the cost of policing regular incidents of low level disorder from other policing activities, chiefly because forces do not separately record this information. Policing disorder is not a discrete heading; as an activity it encompasses a number of areas of policing. This presents problems for activity based costing systems, because it is desirable to have activities that are easily recognisable and can be coded to a particular area. Costing systems are becoming more advanced and the work on developing a standard definition of disorder will assist. Forces will wish to develop this level of costing in order to satisfy their Police Authority and the Government that they are achieving value for money. (HMIC, 1999, p 39)

Despite such guidance, evidence suggests that some forces pay little or no regard to cost issues in relation to the policing of Travelling People. In addition to single encampments, and concerted action such as the example given previously concerning the Thames Valley area, this would include other activities such as the policing of protests at the closure of traditional fairs, such as Horsmonden in Kent in 2000 (see *Travellers' Times*[4], issue 10, December 2000); and creating public order issues where none exist based on assumptions about the behaviour of Travelling People, for example the case of *Smith v Cheltenham Borough Council* (see *Travellers' Times*, issue 8, January 2000). Raids on public Gypsy sites in which a large number of officers are employed against similar or fewer numbers of residents, but following which a few minor charges or no charges at all are laid, would also be an example of related and expensive policing activities (such raids have taken place in Hampshire, Oxfordshire and Coventry in recent years; research on the subject will be forthcoming from the TLRU in 2002/03).

In addition, HMIC reports that police powers of eviction under section 61 of the CJPOA were:

> ... widely used in some areas but not in others. This can lead to frustrations with the local community and landowners that have a perception that a force will take a more active role in dealing with trespass. Her Majesty's Inspector is aware of the concerns and difficulties experienced with some parts of the legislation, particularly in relation to powers to remove trespassers under the Criminal Justice and Public Order Act, but feels strongly that a more robust and consistent approach both within forces and between forces would benefit local partners and the community. This issue is one Her Majesty's Inspector would expect to see reflected in local audits and strategies required under the Crime and Disorder Act. (HMIC, 1999, p 50)

The hard-line approach recommended here by HMIC is both superficial and overly simplistic. It fails to consider Best Value implications and makes no mention of the competing demands of, and pressures on, local authorities, nor the potentially contrary pressures arising from the 1998 Human Rights Act and the 2000 Race Relations (Amendment) Act, which are examined further in the following chapter (it should, however, be noted that the HMIC report just predates the coming into force of these pieces of legislation).

A small number of forces, however, appear to consider that the collection of data, including resource implications, is important when working on the issue of unauthorised encampments.

> The importance of reliable data on police evictions (including an estimate of their cost) was emphasised by many delegates. Chief Inspector Alan Beckley of West Mercia Constabulary commented that it was impossible to estimate the scale of the problem unless accurate records of the operation of statutory powers existed. He pointed to the desirability not only of this specific information being available, but also records of the number of times and under what circumstances statutory powers were not used and landowners were forced to take their own recovery of land action. (Clements and Smith, 1997, p 17)

Obvious and considerable difficulties could be created for local authorities who see unauthorised encampments as a Best Value issue if their local police force takes a different view (and vice versa). The government's own commissioned research recommends that interagency collaboration is essential if unauthorised encampments are to be effectively managed and reduced. The police cannot therefore develop a Best Value approach to unauthorised encampments simply by following HMIC guidance or by working in isolation.

> [N]ew guidance should cover the need for a clear lead agency, with the police taking the lead where there was criminal behaviour or threats and the local authority in other circumstances. All police forces should appoint a liaison officer who would work closely with local authority appointed GTLOs [Gypsy and Traveller Liaison Officers], Gypsies and Travellers and their representative organisations, and contacts with other agencies. (Cowan et al, 2001, p 77)

Best Value would, indeed should, be a useful tool in the development and operation of such a comprehensive, agency-wide approach.

Best Value and unauthorised encampments: a case study

> Economic evaluation is especially useful in considering services at the margin of discretionary spending – it can show what would be gained by expanding budgets, and what is lost by budget cuts. It can show what can be gained by putting more resources into preventative programmes. (Holtermann, 1998, p 43)

In 1999 Dorset County Council produced a *Best Value proposal for environmental services*. In it the authority reported that in recent years it had been developing "a Sensitive Management Strategy for dealing with ... encampments, focusing on resolving potential conflicts through dialogue and negotiation. This strategy has successfully avoided legal costs of up to £1m, and reduced the level of antagonism between travelling and resident communities" (1999, p 19).

The council went on to note that a "high level of trust has been established with the county council's Gypsy and Traveller Liaison Officer [by Travelling People]. This has successfully avoided expensive formal legal action over the last five or six years, saving an estimated £2m in costs of formal legal action and associated measures" (Dorset County Council Environment Services Directorate, 1999, p 3). The estimated £2 million saving created by adopting a Best Value approach in this single authority area can be seen as evidence of the extreme underestimate engendered by the TLRU quantification of the costs of unauthorised encampments.

The history of the relationship of Dorset County Council to unauthorised encampments and issues around Travelling People generally was outlined in the same report in the following terms:

> Dorset was the first county to be designated under the former 1968 Caravan Sites Act. There are permanent gypsy sites at Coldharbour in Wareham, Piddlehinton near Dorchester, Thornicombe near Blandford, a small site near Shaftesbury and currently a closed site at Mannington Park. The active sites provide 53 pitches including 4 transit pitches.
>
> The County Council implements a policy of sensitive management in relation to unauthorised encampments. It does not take action on behalf of private landowners but will liaise with gypsies and travellers who may be encamped

on private land on behalf of a private landowner in order to negotiate a mutually acceptable solution. Private landowners are advised that should they wish to invoke legal proceedings in order to remove gypsies or travellers that they should make their own arrangements to do so.

Unauthorised encampments on county, district or borough council land are all managed in the first instance by the County Council's Gypsy and Traveller Liaison Officer who will seek to obtain assurances and commitments from the travellers as to their intentions and to agree mutually acceptable periods of occupation depending upon the use of the land and the extent and degree of any nuisance....

This balanced approach has avoided the need for formal legal action with associated costs. Notwithstanding this, the County Council has worked in partnership with in particular, North Dorset District Council, in the use of legal action to address unauthorised encampments on a large scale on St James Common.

The consistent application of this sensitive management policy has resulted in:

- Considerable financial savings to the County Council.
- A marked reduction in the number of complaints from members of the public.
- An increased level of understanding and trust between the public authorities and travellers which has ensured that:
  - Gypsy and traveller groups who may have encamped on sensitive sites move on more quickly by mutual agreement.
  - Gypsy and traveller groups remain on less sensitive sites for extended periods by mutual agreement.

Contrary to concerns expressed by authorities during the Birmingham research study, in Dorset's experience the policy of sensitive management has contributed to a reduction in the number and frequency of unauthorised encampments and has not caused a 'honey-pot' effect.

This is a local authority that sees unauthorised encampments as a Best Value issue, and did so even before the 1999 Local Government Act came into force, anticipating both the Best Value regime and the *Good practice guide* on managing unauthorised encampments.

Following the publication of the *Good practice guide* in 1998, the Council undertook a review of its policy. Again, this review preceded Best Value but was in many ways similar to the approach Best Value requires. Firstly, an 'issues' report was published, including an assessment of the effectiveness of policies and procedures as against the *Guide*, with key issues expressed in the form of questions (the 'challenge' function that would come to be required in Best Value). Views were sought from the police authority, district and borough councils, other agencies, Gypsies and Travellers and the public generally, and voluntary organisations such as Friends, Families and Travellers and the Children's Society (anticipating the Best Value 'consult' element).

Some of the results of the consultation were that: current permanent site provision met the needs of Gypsies but not other Travellers; the sensitive management approach was consistent with government guidelines; restricting access by larger groups to council land and leaving areas for smaller family groups was generally considered a balanced approach (although not all consultees agreed); existing formal liaison arrangements were inadequate; regional arrangements should be re-established; councils should provide temporary stopping places; and that the multi-agency approach was working well. There was mixed feedback on the provision of facilities for unauthorised encampments, the response to nuisance and the need for further provision of information to all interested parties.

An independent MORI survey was also carried out in the council area at around the same time, to ascertain the priorities of area residents with respect to spending allocation. Spending on Gypsy and Traveller services was the lowest priority identified. Therefore, if in future the council wished to alter its 'sensitive management' policy in favour of a more enforcement-style approach to unauthorised encampments, it would have to 1) acknowledge that such a change might cost extra money, perhaps as much as £1 million per annum; and 2) identify budgets from which such increased expenditure might be drawn. The MORI survey provided clear evidence that this outcome is not one that local residents would support.

Dorset acknowledges that its Best Value approach does not always work. There were setbacks in that there was an increase in the numbers of Travellers (and size of groups of Travellers) residing in the county following the solar eclipse in the summer of 1999. Some encampments had stayed for increased lengths of times on particular unauthorised locations, and in 2000 it proved more difficult to negotiate leaving dates with some of the residents of these encampments. There were new groups with whom no rapport had been established, and established groups who saw the Council as committing a breach of faith by closing off long-standing stopping places on land sold off for capital receipts.

So what is next for the county in this area? A Member Scrutiny Group of five councillors was set up in 2000 to carry out further consultation, review policy and make recommendations for change. There is political support for temporary stopping places, which are already being identified, and a scheme for Shaftesbury Common has been implemented whereby large group access will be restricted but informal areas can be used by smaller groups for temporary stays.

Dorset County Council has, through thoughtful and focused policy development around unauthorised encampments, created a unique situation in relation to encampments and Best Value. Were the sensitive management policy to be changed, the Council would have to make an overt decision about where funding and resources would come from to cope with the increased legal and other action that would almost certainly follow. That is, there would have to be formal recognition and quantification of the costs of not providing sites or operating a 'toleration' policy. This is consistent with the Audit Commission's recommendations: to identify, explore and choose between alternatives based on specified, necessary and positive outcomes.

The links between Best Value, and the processes followed and actions taken by Dorset County Council, are evident. There has been challenge in the issues report and ongoing review. Consultation has been undertaken and will continue to take place around Traveller-related issues. Comparisons have been made with developments in other local authority areas and with other research (for example, the *Good practice guide*) and will continue to be made (that is, with this TLRU research and forthcoming government research). Continuous improvements are being sought and made in this area of the authority's work. Best Value is not seen as a threat, but as an opportunity.

During the July 2000 TLRU seminar on Best Value and unauthorised encampments, the Head of Business Support for the Environmental Services Directorate in the County of Dorset, Mr David Ayre, was questioned from the floor concerning his Council's policy. These questions and his answers provide further information concerning the approach taken by this local authority, and can be found in Appendix F. Mr Ayre stated that: "All of this has been hard work and will continue to require tenacity and commitment, but it is seen as necessary work through which benefits outweigh burdens in the long and the short term".

Unauthorised encampments: a Best Value issue

The Best Value programme can easily, and should, be applied to authorised sites for Travelling People. For instance, Milton Keynes Council resolved to use some of the residue of its 2000 Housing Investment Programme (HIP) budget to connect its Willen Travellers Site to mains drainage, as it estimated that this would save about £14,000 per year in charges for emptying the existing septic tank. Because the septic tank costs were previously met from the 'Traveller budget', the Council estimated that in subsequent years they should be able to use this money to meet other needs of Travelling People. This is in keeping both with the principles of Best Value, and Community and Race Relations best practice.

Equally, respondents to the TLRU costs survey suggest that they may be prepared to approach unauthorised encampments in a fair and financially responsible manner. "The approach of toleration where possible is much cheaper than swift movement where not necessary". Some authorities even suggested useful approaches: "Much of our work at the moment is in looking at long-term solutions. This includes media work to eliminate the stereotyped image of nomadic people. We use liaison as the prime solution, resorting to eviction only as a last resort".

Yet other local authorities persist in seeing the costs of unauthorised encampments as something outside Best Value considerations; as a simple matter of blaming Travelling People for a lack of suitable and lawful stopping places. There are some reasonable arguments to justify such an approach in relation to behaviour; that is, in relation to the minority of Travelling People who consistently and unjustifiably leave a trail of devastation in their wake. This is no different than fining individual dog owners for not clearing up after their pets in public spaces rather than levy charges on all dog owners regardless of behaviour. However, some authorities generalise rather more than this. For instance, one respondent to the TLRU survey said:

> Currently it is impossible to recover any costs from the occupiers. Perhaps consideration should be given to strengthening the law to discourage such occupation, to make recovery of possession easier where unlawful occupation occurs and to perhaps allow seizure of the travellers assets (such as caravans) until all costs incurred by the Council have been paid.

In the climate of clear and widespread accounting occasioned by the new Best Value regime, it is a matter of some concern that such substantial sums as those identified in this study do not undergo formal budgeting or recording. It has already been noted how few of the costs associated with unauthorised encampments were 'counted' at all. Only 26% of 229 authorities (59) had any sort of budget for responding to encampments, and only a handful of these budgets fell under specific headings; the remainder came from general departmental and/or contingency budgets. Evidently unauthorised encampments are for the most part not yet considered, at a local level, as an issue to which the pursuit of economy, efficiency and effectiveness applies. As an example, one local authority expressed the view that the costs of encampments are related to their number, yet did not appear to perceive a role for Best Value:

> Costs such as salaries, fuel, court fees, rise continually, but other costs connected with unauthorised encampments include the amount of time spent in dealing with them eg site visits, meetings with local residents, telephone calls, correspondence, media and so on which, obviously, depend on [the] size or nuisance of each encampment and are impossible to evaluate. Only fewer encampments will reduce costs.

Some respondents to the TLRU costs survey indicated that they do see encampments in 'value for money' terms, even if they did not express such views by reference to Best Value. For instance, one respondent commented: "In the days when circumstances did dictate that we took action we discovered that the costs were disproportionate to the benefits gained". The 2001 AGM of the National Association of Gypsy and Traveller Officers (NAGTO) was themed 'Human Rights Best Value'; and a course on 'Gypsies and Travellers: Policy and Provision', run by the South West Provincial Employers organisation in Taunton in March 2001, included in its programme a Best Value workshop.

Northampton Borough Council has gone further in formally linking the issue of unauthorised encampments to its Best Value regime. 'Encampments' are deemed to be a 'service', and the Council's Best Value Performance Plan 2000/01 describes the service area as scoring highly, in terms of the assessment criteria for the Best Value review timetable, "on community importance, its linkages with the Borough's Community Plan and the fact that it provides a partnership theme. This service requires close working with other partners (Police, County Council) and can be classed as a cross-cutting theme" (Northampton Borough Council, 2001, p 1).

In January 2001 the Council completed and published the results of a review of encampments by its Best Value review team. The review took as its starting point the statistical and budgetary implications of dealing with unauthorised encampments:

- £424,000 was spent between 1995 and 1999 on moving Travellers and clearing sites;
- 60% of all encampments related to three families;
- more was spent since 1995 per head of population on moving Travellers than on air pollution, health promotion or communicative disease control;
- complaints about Travellers and unauthorised encampments were 2.5 times higher than any other single aspect of environmental health;
- 'bunding' ('protection') of land had reduced available sites and numbers of encampments, but the result was a core group of Travellers who did not move out of town but who 'recirculated'.

The review team found that the 'true costs' of dealing with unauthorised encampments were not accurately reflected in the Council's service budgets; some costs were hidden within other services or Directorates. The team also considered the 'human costs' to evictees an important matter to be taken into consideration when assessing costs overall. Under the 'compare' element of Best Value, it was found that costs comparisons with other local authorities were difficult to obtain as most were unable to give specific budget details.

Nonetheless, the team was able to conclude, among other things, that "Best Value does not support the non-toleration of unauthorised encampments. The costs of eviction will continue to rise if alternatives to the cycle of evictions within the town [including site provision] are not pursued". (However, consultation with the local settled community established that 67% were not prepared for council tax to be increased to pay for future options.) The full executive summary of the review's outcome can be seen in Appendix G.

For those local authorities, such as Northampton Borough Council, that do decide that the policy for encampments is relevant to their Best Value programme, there are a number of practical factors that at present may militate against including encampment-related spending in a Best Value programme. It is clear from the response of many councils that, because there is no central budget for managing encampments, costs are spread between different departments and therefore may go uncounted or be difficult to count. (One district council stated that: "Members dislike contingency budgets so actual budgets are shrinking; reliance is placed on virements".)

Additionally, it may be difficult to define 'inputs, outputs and outcomes' in respect of unauthorised encampments, and to build Best Value into an area that is highly unpredictable. One respondent stated that: "A major encampment could easily recur in the district and could still give rise to potentially huge costs in view of the procedures involved and risk of challenge".

Nonetheless, Northampton and Dorset Councils have shown that Best Value can be a useful and usable tool in this context. Other local authorities may at any rate be forced to find ways of overcoming any difficulties they may confront in building Best Value and the balancing of rights and interests into encampment 'services'. A large proportion of the overall population of Travelling People fall within the categories 'Gypsy' or 'Irish Traveller', and both groups have been recognised by case law as falling under the protection of race relations legislation. The law in this area is quickly expanding and placing ever more onerous requirements and balancing acts on local authorities, a theme that is explored further in the next chapter.

Notes

[1] Information from the UK government website at www.open.gov.uk/

[2] This and most other Audit Commission publications are available at www.audit-commission.gov.uk/

[3] 1986 Public Order Act, which police powers of eviction were replaced by section 61 of the 1994 CJPOA.

[4] The *Travellers' Times* magazine, TLRU, Cardiff Law School available at www.cf.ac.uk/claws/tlru/TT.html.

SIX

Rights, race relations and Best Value

The 1998 Human Rights Act

Only two respondent authorities to the TLRU costs survey mentioned the 1998 Human Rights Act (HRA). One authority referred to it in the context of reviewing policies relating to unauthorised encampments in order to ensure the authority's compliance with the Act. The other suggested that landowners and businesses might have a remedy for the costs and disruption they incur in relation to encampments, under Protocol 1, Article 1 of the Convention (the right to peaceful enjoyment of possessions).

The principles and structure of the Best Value regime demand that the implications of the Act be taken into account by public bodies. The HRA came into force in the UK on 2 October 2000[1], and incorporates the European Convention on Human Rights (ECHR) into British law. The Convention rights and freedoms protected under the HRA include Article 6, the right to a fair trial; Article 8, the right to respect for private and family life, home and correspondence; Article 11, the right to freedom of assembly and association; and Article 14, the prohibition of discrimination on any ground such as sex, race, colour, language, religion, opinion, national or social origin, association with a national minority, property, birth or other status. Also included within the HRA are the rights under the various Protocols (ECHR supplements) to which the UK is a party, including the right to peaceful enjoyment of possessions (Protocol 1, Article 1), and the right to education (Protocol 1, Article 2).

Probably the most unique feature of Article 14 is that the grounds on which discrimination are claimed may not be as important as the fact that discrimination has taken place. The list of grounds is not exhaustive and other grounds have been held to be acceptable (for example, age and sexual orientation). For example, this may reduce long-standing legal argument about what does or does not constitute a 'Gypsy'; a complainant may not have to show that they are a Gypsy but only that they were treated in an unjustifiably discriminatory way because it was believed that they were.

Police services and local authorities are counselled by the government to review their policies and practices, with a view to ensuring that these are HRA compliant. The Act is aimed by government at respecting and fostering Convention rights in everything a public authority does. Therefore, all public authorities have a positive obligation to ensure that respect for human rights is at the core of all of their work, acting in a way that positively reinforces the principles of the Act. The HRA supports this by making it unlawful for a public authority to act (or fail to act) in a way that is incompatible with a Convention right.

This covers all aspects of public authority activities, including drafting rules, regulations and bylaws; internal personnel matters; administrative procedures; all forms and instances of decision making; the implementation of policy; and an authority's relationship with members of the public.

> Respect for Convention rights should be at the very heart of everything you do. If your organisation's existing procedures are not compatible, it will need to implement new policies and procedures which are consistent with the Convention rights. You should consider how the relevant parts of the Act apply to all aspects of your work, and be able to show that you have done so. You should be able to justify your decisions in the context of the Convention rights, and show that you have considered the Convention rights and dealt with any issues arising out of such a consideration.

> You also need to think about how, and the extent to which, the laws underpinning your policies and procedures could help you do more to build a culture of rights and responsibilities. There may be issues here to discuss with the senior manager of your organisation and with a sponsoring government department.

> In your day to day work you have a crucial human rights role to play, not only in ensuring that you always act in accordance with the Convention rights, but also in supporting a positive attitude to human rights issues throughout the community. (Home Office, 2000, pp 16-17)

The HRA is not a charter for the prevention of evictions of Travelling People, but it does require public bodies to review and justify how they take decisions and what decisions they reach. This is a fundamental change in the way in which authorities operate: before the HRA, public bodies were only required to ensure that they reached their decisions in a lawful manner, but the merits of decisions could not generally be challenged.

A Local Government Association Planning Committee working paper on *Gypsy/Traveller issues* (LGAPC, 1997) expresses concern in relation to potential increased legal costs, because it believes that the incorporation of the ECHR "will certainly have implications for gypsies' rights on the basis that they are classified as an ethnic group. There is the likelihood in particular that their treatment under the 1994 [CJPO] Act could be the subject of renewed challenge in the courts" (1997, paragraph 10). The TLRU is undertaking research during 2001/02 into the impact of the HRA on local authorities and Travelling People.

Responses to the TLRU costs survey suggest that not all local authorities are aware of the implications of the HRA in respect of unauthorised encampments. For example, one respondent justified its (unwritten) 'zero tolerance' policy by reference to the will of 'local people', the existence of which they explained as follows:

I think that travellers are seen as one group, rather than recognising the different sub-groups that exist … a sort of mobile underclass if you will. The community has enough problems with its resident underclass that it feels it can do little about so the appearance of a travelling underclass presents an opportunity to remove them in the way that the wider society would like to remove other groups. Any council, and I am sure this applies to this one, will therefore seek to follow the wishes of the community it represents.

In seeking to meet the approval of such (assumed) views without question, this authority does not appear to be acting in a manner that fairly balances the rights and freedoms of different people. It may thereby be acting unlawfully, and risking increased costs in relation to unauthorised encampments in the form of legal challenges to its approach. (As can be seen in Table 3.2, ten respondents to this study indicated their belief that costs are increasing because Travelling People are becoming ever more inclined to know and assert their rights; and 12 because legal costs in particular are increasing.)

Of course, this respondent might, in the short term, see the additional legal costs of non-compliance with the HRA as a price worth paying for local accord. Although the quoted authority does see a costs issue being raised by its approach, it also comments that it would rather the costs be paid by the public body than by others. "There are those costs borne by landowners, residents and the local community in respect of disruption, crime and the fear of crime. We do not see ourselves moving towards greater tolerance at the cost of social disruption". It is very possible, then, that the threat of legal challenge to its policy and practice would be insufficient in itself to alter the way in which this local authority handles unauthorised encampments.

The Race Relations Acts

A TLRU respondent noted that the most widespread attitude towards Travelling People in his/her area was typified by the following comment:"I've no objection to the real Romanies, the true gypsies, but these people are not true gypsies and they must be prevented from living this sort of life in this area". This focus on 'bloodedness' does seem to be common: similar remarks were uncovered in looking at the reform of the Caravan Sites Act (see Chapter Two). It is also deeply flawed, irrational, racist and not applied to other minority groups in the UK.

It is certainly unlikely that many of the travellers today are pure-blooded descendants of those wandering people of Indian origin who first came to this country some five hundred years ago, since a considerable amount of 'marrying-out' has taken place.... Nevertheless, it is probable that most of today's travellers have some Romany blood. And all, irrespective of the extent of their Romany blood, experience the same difficulties in carrying on their way of life in our society. (Ministry of Housing and Local Government/ Welsh Office, 1967, p 43)

Despite the difficulties inherent in pinning any individual down to some 'pure' category of racial or national origin, some groups in the UK are recognised as being minority ethnic groups under legislation that purports to offer them protection from ill treatment resulting from membership of those groups. The 1976 Race Relations Act (RRA) deems it unlawful for certain public and private service-providing bodies to discriminate, directly or indirectly, or victimise on the basis of racial origin.

The question of which groups should be protected under this Act has been determined by the courts on a case-by-case basis. Gypsies have been so protected since 1989 (*Commission for Racial Equality v Dutton* [1989] 1 QB 783) and Irish Travellers only recently. The 1997 Race Relations (Northern Ireland) Order section 5(2)(a) states that 'racial grounds' includes the grounds of belonging to the Irish Traveller community. That is to say, "the community of people commonly so called who are identified (both by themselves and others) as people with a shared history, culture and traditions including, historically, a nomadic way of life on the Island of Ireland". (The Order goes on to state, in section 5(3), that the term 'racial group' includes the Irish Traveller community.) In addition, a judicial decision in London in August 2000 established that Irish Travellers are a 'racial group' for the purposes of the 1976 Act in Britain (*P.O'Leary and Others v Allied Domecq and Others* [2000] Central London County Court 29 August No CL 950275-79).

As an example of the protection available under the Act, in 1990 a Gypsy claimant living on an unauthorised encampment was told that she could not receive any further payment of income support and severe disablement allowance until she moved to an authorised site. The claimant asked for and received such a requirement in writing, and the Commission for Racial Equality (CRE) was then able to issue proceedings under the RRA sections 20 and 21 – discrimination in the provision of goods and services – on her behalf. The Department of Social Security settled the case without liability and paid damages and costs (*Welfare Rights Bulletin*, No 105, December 1991, p 11).

Some of the comments provided to the TLRU as part of the costs questionnaire show a lack of awareness that many Travelling People could be considered members of minority ethnic groups. As has been noted, one respondent stated its belief that the way of life of Travelling People is a "totally unjustified burden on local council taxpayers, robbing them of services which could otherwise be provided". The respondent added that 'travelling' "is a parasitic lifestyle". Yet another respondent stated:

> It appears that the romantic nature of the Romany Traveller has now disappeared in urban areas and that authorities are left with what have been described as 'itinerant travellers/tinkers'. The perception of these by local people is not good, they can only be seen in their eyes as troublemakers, up to no good. [This] Council is currently looking at ways of reducing costs by restricting the commercial productivity of sites by travellers. We are considering employment of security guards and provision of basic amenities in order to encourage travellers to keep a cleaner site and possibly move on of their own volition.

Other quotes from the responses to this research also suggest an approach in which the separation of Travelling and 'settled' communities is seen as desirable and/or unavoidable (except where conventional housing is used by all). One authority operates a policy little different from the abolished 'designation' scheme (see Chapter Two): "Since authorised sites have been established, [the] toleration policy has been lifted".

Another respondent appears to suggest that difficulties Travelling People have pursuing their way of life in the face of such policies and attitudes is leading to the diminution of 'Travelling'; it believes costs to be decreasing because of the "unavailability of traditional camping grounds and increased tendency by Travellers to accept house tenancies". Yet another authority acknowledged that they had made it more difficult for Gypsies to lawfully attend a traditional social and economic event of long standing: "The greatest cost incurred by the Council is in respect of Gypsies travelling to [major annual event]. Unfortunately it was not possible to provide an official site for 1999 and therefore most of the encampments were unauthorised".

There is evidence, from this and other research, that attitudes clearly not compliant with the spirit and letter of the RRA often stem from other 'local' people, to whom the authorities must respond. One respondent to the TLRU stated that: "A [county]-wide policy of toleration of encampments for 2 to 3 weeks has saved considerable officer and legal costs; although local residents often call for immediate eviction". And a London borough reported to TLRU that: "In the eyes of the public the success of the Council is measured in preventing Traveller encampments, the speed of eviction and the speed of returning the land fit for its normal use". Some local authorities obviously have a difficult task at times in balancing the interests, beliefs and perceived needs of Travelling and non-Travelling communities; still others do not apparently endeavour to strike such a balance.

Race relations legislation has recently been considerably amended and strengthened, making it even more important that local authorities and the police do not pander to knee-jerk, anti-Travelling views but find ways of improving tolerance and understanding between different communities in their areas. The 1976 Race Relations Act, as amended by the 2000 Race Relations (Amendment) Act, makes it unlawful for any public body, or any body carrying out a public function (a broad definition of 'public body' also employed under the 1998 Human Rights Act), to discriminate while carrying out any of its functions. The amended Act also imposes a positive duty on all major public bodies (named in a schedule to the Act, as identified by the Home Secretary, including all local authorities) to promote equality of opportunity and good race relations in the performance of their functions.

Public bodies may therefore no longer be able to allow viewpoints such as those quoted to dictate unquestioningly their policy and practice in relation to unauthorised encampments, at least where certain groups of Travelling People are concerned. As with the Human Rights Act, this race equality legislation presents those authorities that pursue eviction of encampments as a matter of course with a quandary. It may be seen as being in keeping with Best Value to follow what is perceived to be the 'local' (anti-Travelling) view, but this view may not be sustainable if legal and other challenges result from non-compliance with important new obligations as to rights and community and race relations[3].

Best Value and race relations

Due to the precedence given to improving community and race relations (CRR) in the UK in the wake of the murder of Stephen Lawrence and resultant inquiry (links to the inquiry report and related documents are at www.homeoffice.gov.uk), measures taken by public bodies to attain such improvement through service delivery will be under scrutiny in the years to come. Local government is expected to work at identifying and countering institutionalised discrimination within their departments and in their service delivery, a problem defined by the Stephen Lawrence Inquiry as "the collective failure of an organisation to provide an appropriate and professional service to people because of their colour, culture, or ethnic origin" (MacPherson, 1999, para 6.34).

The Employers' Organisation for Local Government (EO), through its internet pages at www.lg-employers.gov.uk, provides councils with information designed to assist them in the development of "a comprehensive approach to addressing racial inequality in employment and service delivery". The resource also aims to:

> ... assist councils to embed racial equality issues into mainstream policies and practices. Where possible we have used information and good practice examples that combine work on the Stephen Lawrence Inquiry with meeting the government's racial equality Best Value performance indicators, preparing for the likely requirements of the new Race Relations Act and the wider equalities agenda. (www.lg-employers.gov.uk/)

Forty of the recommendations arising from the Stephen Lawrence Inquiry are deemed by the EO to be relevant to local government, distilled into three essential lessons. Local authorities must learn the need to: examine the outcomes of the council's policies and procedures for black, Asian and minority ethnic people; increase the involvement of black, Asian and minority ethnic people in the council; and ensure that everyone in the council (and its partners) recognises and acts on their responsibilities to change the culture of the council and its community to one that tackles racism and racial inequality and promotes racial equality.

The EO, the Local Government Association and the Improvement and Development Agency (IDeA) suggest that local government can meet the concerns raised by the Stephen Lawrence Inquiry by taking at least seven actions to address race equality issues:

• use the CRE Standard to review progress, produce a policy statement and develop an action plan to address institutional racism;

- mainstream racial equality into Best Value work;
- develop an effective racial equality training programme;
- deal with complaints of racial discrimination and harassment;
- address racial inequality in employment;
- champion a commitment to racial equality and cultural diversity;
- evaluate progress.

The most direct impact on local government as a result of government emphasis on race equality issues – aside from amendments to race relations law – has been the introduction of relevant Best Value Performance Indicators (BVPIs). The BVPIs introduced by the DETR and the Audit Commission for 2000/01 include at least 29 that relate to racial equality issues (see Appendix H, where these are reproduced by permission).

Four corporate health (national) indicators focus on these issues: the CRE Standard, workforce monitoring, measuring customer satisfaction and classifying complaints by ethnicity. Under the 1999 LGA, local authorities have a legal obligation to collect this information and their responses form an important part of Best Value inspections. If an authority's attainment is thought to be unsatisfactory, the Audit Commission can make recommendations to the Secretary of State for amendments to the authority's performance plans.

A key BVPI is the obligation for local authorities to measure themselves against the Commission for Racial Equality (CRE, 1998) *Racial equality means quality* Standard. The Standard was first published in 1995 and sets out a framework for improving race equality performance in policy and planning, service delivery, community development, employment and corporate image. It can be used by authorities to help them produce a policy statement, develop an action plan and review progress.

The level of CRE Standard attained depends on the stage reached by an authority in incorporating racial equality into its policy and practice. Levels 1 and 2 are about developing policy statements and action plans; levels 3 and 4 relate to improvements that should happen as a result of implementing the policies; and level 5 is only for those councils that are national leaders in achieving racial equality. Through the auspices of the Best Value regime, local authorities must state which level of the Standard they have reached in the area of service provision, having audited all of their departments to establish which level each has attained. The department that has attained the lowest level sets the level for the entire authority.

The "linking of the Standard to the DETR and Audit Commission's performance indicators, and the development of racial equality as the subject of corporate health indicators under Best Value, emphasise the relationship between quality and equality" (London Borough of Hammersmith and Fulham, 2001, p 15). In 2000 the Local Government Association, EO and CRE commissioned the London Borough of Hammersmith and Fulham to undertake a survey of progress on adoption and implementation of the CRE Standard in English councils, 90% of which responded. Seventy percent of respondents had adopted the Standard, but of these only 40% had yet carried out an audit.

The report of the CRE Standard survey therefore identified three main areas of concern. First, that many of the authorities that had adopted the Standard had not carried out audits. Second, an authority is unlikely to be able to identify the level it has reached without carrying out such an audit. Additionally, over 40% of district councils had not yet adopted the Standard.

> Many of them have small minority ethnic populations and possibly believe that the Standard is not relevant to their situation. Nevertheless, these authorities will be expected to comply with the new public duty to promote racial equality in the Race Relations (Amendment) Act. Early adoption and implementation of the Standard will help councils to prepare for their new responsibilities, by providing a framework for auditing their performance....

> There appear to be striking differences in the levels achieved within individual authorities; for example only one council achieved level four of the Standard overall whereas nine councils had individual departments at this level. This suggests that there is considerable scope for departments or services within a council to learn from each other. In some authorities, resources could be directed at under-performing departments or directorates to bring them up to the level of the best. (London Borough of Hammersmith and Fulham, 2001, p 22)

Her Majesty's Inspectorate of Constabulary (HMIC), through its *Winning the race* programme, has investigated the extent to which police forces are incorporating CRR within their five-year programme of Best Value reviews. In 2000 HMIC recorded its disappointment that nine forces had not done so. "The comparison and consultative elements within the disciplines of Best Value present an ideal setting for checking and developing the quality of service to minorities. The disappointment is more acute when the APA [Association of Police Authorities] recommend that the needs of diversity are built into all Best Value reviews" (HMIC, 2000, p 97).

The Best Value and CRR regimes are still in the early stages of development and implementation. The research to date suggests that it will be some time yet before these programmes are integrated into local policy and practice. In the 2001 report on the Audit Commission expectations from year two of Best Value, the Commission expressed concern that too many Best Value reviews focused on specific services rather than cross-cutting issues, "which does not serve to connect Best Value with the promotion of economic and social well-being" (2001a, p 7). Many authorities were found to employ the Best Value tool to confirm the status quo or deliver change only incrementally. And many authorities pursued Best Value "as competing with, not complementing, regeneration and social inclusion strategies".

Research for the IDeA suggests that, while most local authorities think it important to 'join up' Best Value with a plethora of other recent initiatives, most are struggling to do so. Very few local authorities surveyed through the study identified equality, rights or inclusion-related initiatives as among the most essential (Cowell et al, 2001). This is not surprising, since, unlike Best Value, rights legislation and CRR initiatives have not been linked to formal structures or systems of objectives and evaluation.

Nonetheless, the frameworks for the integration of these programmes are explicit, comprehensive and mandatory. It is likely that, over time, progress in the spheres of Best Value and CRR will come to be looked upon and dealt with by all local authorities as linked, inbuilt and measurable. Ample guidance exists to assist local authorities in this work and a significant number of organisations – including the CRE, EO, IDeA, Local Government Association and Audit Commission – exist to aid and direct it.

In addition to the Best Value regime, the Local Government Act places a duty on local authorities to prepare a community strategy to promote or improve the economic, social and environmental well-being of their areas (bringing together local authorities, agencies and private and voluntary sectors into strategic partnerships to plan and deliver the steps necessary to improve all of these aspects of local quality of life). The DETR (2000b) noted, in its report *Quality and choice: A decent home for all*, that housing "is a key element in determining quality of life. The housing strategies produced by local authorities should therefore form an important component of the broader community strategies drawn up under the 2000 Act" (see www.housing.odpm.gov.uk). It is not yet certain whether sites, and lack of sites, will come to be regarded and approached by partnerships (and their overseers) as an issue belonging within this strategy; and, if not, how this will be justified in the context of race equality obligations.

Central government and local services

Many police forces and police organisations are working towards approaches to unauthorised encampments and Travelling People that are in keeping with the terms of the HRA and race relations law; particularly since and in response to the 1998 Stephen Lawrence Inquiry's identification of 'institutionalised racism' as a problem within the police service. For example, the Association of Chief Police Officers (ACPO) Community and Race Relations Committee has a 'portfolio' group on Gypsies and Travellers, preparing a guide to understanding and working with those communities for use in 2002.

However, these moves towards better CRR may be complicated by the Home Office, which is responsible for overseeing the operation both of police powers and race relations. The Home Office Statement of Purpose is: "To build a safe, just and tolerant society in which the rights and responsibilities of individuals, families and communities are properly balanced and the protection and security of the public are maintained". And yet, as noted in the previous chapter, the department appears to want the police to take a firmer stand against unauthorised encampments.

The apparent lead given by the Home Office to police services, whether consciously or not, is that unauthorised encampments (and the people living on them) are not viewed as a matter that attracts either Best Value or race relations and equal opportunities considerations. In its annual report on *Race equality in public services*, the department frequently conflates 'race' with 'colour' (Home Office Communication Directorate, 2000, 2001). Both the 2000 and 2001 documents include on the opening page the statement that the government is committed to "creating a country where 'every colour is a good colour', where 'everyone is treated according to their rights and needs' and 'where racial diversity is celebrated".

Page 7 of the 2000 report states it to be "essential that the Government drive to improve public service includes the delivery of appropriate public services to minority ethnic groups. To achieve this the Government needs to know what the position is now, and whether and where improvements need to be made". The range of 'performance management networks' quoted (on page 9) as tools to improve race equality include the Best Value regime.

However, the Home Office notes that, for the purposes of these documents, the term 'ethnic minorities' refers only to those from the black and Asian communities living in Britain. In fact, there is no express or implicit indication in any of the documents available to public bodies in respect of either Best Value or race relations law, by any central government department or other body, that unauthorised encampments or Travelling People are to be included in such considerations.

The Audit Commission's (1999) briefing paper *Listen up! Effective community consultation* examines the process in the context of Best Value. In the executive summary of this paper (on page 8), a graph shows that authorities find some groups harder to consult than others. Ninety percent of authorities reported difficulties in consulting homeless people; roughly 75% in respect of young people; around 67% in relation to minority ethnic groups; and 75% were found to have difficulty 'reaching' Travellers. As the Audit Commission identifies Travelling People as a group to consult, it may be looking to see that consultation has been attempted as it examines how authorities are meeting their 1999 LGA duties.

However, most of the focuses and measures suggested to local authorities by the Audit Commission, including BVPIs, are not relevant to Travelling People and/or are exclusive of them, that is, the emphasis is on fixed housing. In 1998 the TLRU asked the Commission whether it would be interested in undertaking an analysis of the costs of not providing sites. A Commission officer stated that, while the issue was an interesting one, the sums involved were too low to justify research work by a busy national department (a statement which could be viewed as putting one of the major justifications for the 1994 legal reforms into question).

Whether the Audit Commission will focus on unauthorised encampments and/or Travelling People through the Best Value mechanism is therefore difficult to assess at present. Certainly, in its 2001 report on the development of Best Value – in which it concludes that almost two thirds of English and Welsh councils are still either 'coasting' or providing poor services 18 months after the Best Value duty came into being – the Commission makes no mention of

CRR or equality issues (Audit Commission, 2001b). The report encourages greater use of reviews on cross-cutting issues, unauthorised encampments having been identified as one such issue by Northampton Borough Council in its Best Value review (see Chapter Five).

During 2001/02, the CRE is drafting and issuing guidance to various public bodies on how to approach and meet the new race relations requirements. It remains to be seen whether it will include Travelling People or other less 'visible' minorities, either overtly or by inference, in such guidance. The TLRU has been asked by the CRE to provide advice on draft documents in this respect, but has not, as of spring 2002, been sent any such drafts for consultation.

It appears that currently local authorities and police services are not encouraged by central government or regulatory bodies to include unauthorised encampments and the people on them within Best Value and race relations projects. Some public bodies have done so and others may in the near future.

Nevertheless, in light of remarks made by some TLRU respondents, and the lack of formal accounting or policies indicated in the majority of responses to the TLRU research, Best Value and CRR will only be included in the encampment 'tool kit' by many public bodies when they are actively made to do so. Even an authority such as Northampton Borough Council, which has included encampments in its Best Value programme, has not done so in a way that overtly includes considerations of equality, inclusion or CRR.

The government insists, through the imposition of the Best Value regime, that local authorities learn from the past and work towards a more efficient and effective future: "It is clear that the Best Value regime will need to continue to evolve at national and local levels. It will therefore be important to be able to reflect upon and learn from the on-going experience of implementing Best Value initiatives" (Martin et al, 1999, p 124).

The DETR makes it clear that the duty of Best Value is "one that local authorities will owe to local people, both as taxpayers and users, and that it is intended to apply to all local authority services" (1998, paragraph 2.1). But it is central government that will continue to set the basic framework for service provision, including national standards.

The Housing Directorate of the ODPM has responsibility for homelessness, local authority housing management, Best Value in housing and tenant participation, and 'Gypsies'; the latter two are treated within the unit as separate matters. The department, in its Green Paper on reforming UK housing (DETR, 2000b), uses words such as 'all' and 'everyone' a great many times, yet – as the reform proposals are 'bricks and mortar' focused – the only people in the UK to whom the promises of the paper do not apply are Travelling People (and asylum seekers).

There is no duty of Best Value on central government and no supra-Audit Commission to assess whether one national policy on a particular issue is better than another. Central government departments cannot seem to agree on the approach to unauthorised encampments; in practice, this can leave local authorities and police services uncertain as to the proper course of action, and Travelling People living in a highly uncertain atmosphere day to day, depending on which area they are in. The contradiction between enforcement and social welfare messages and functions can place public bodies and their officers in difficult positions.

However, while governmental action and inaction colour what local authorities and police are able to do, it does not absolve local public bodies of their obligations and responsibilities. There are those who recognise the need to 'get on with it' as best they can.

One local authority that returned the TLRU questionnaire expressed its belief that: "Until Central Government gives direction to the issue of accommodation within the travelling community, local authorities will be left to deal with the problem in isolation and pay the bill". Be that as it may, while authorities may not be able to avoid experiencing and responding to encampments in their areas, obligations and opportunities are being presented to them through new legislation that can be employed either to raise or help to manage the costs of doing so. It is a matter of choice on the part of each local public body which path it takes (although the stance taken by their neighbouring bodies will also influence the incidence of encampments and therefore possibly also the approach to them).

One authority has this to say:

> It is clear that no local authority can resolve the issues relating to Travellers in isolation and that a regional or national approach is needed.... Local authorities who do not follow acknowledged good practice in their dealings with Travellers leave themselves vulnerable to judicial challenge. However, local authorities are given no incentive to provide sites or pursue policies of toleration. Indeed those that do either by providing sites or by pursuing policies of toleration could initially become a magnet for Travellers seeking refuge from more draconian policies being pursued elsewhere. Thus there is a built-in inertia that may cause some local authorities to go slow or mark time in their policy development. Unless progress is made, however, the expensive cycle of continual eviction from one place to the next will be perpetuated. (Wealden District Council, 2000, p 14)

The policies and objectives in the Best Value strategy of an authority may include such issues and phrases as 'social inclusion', 'social justice' or 'equal opportunities', which will necessitate the inclusion of Travelling People if the meeting of these ideals is to be realistic and properly monitored. For those local authorities that wish to behave equitably towards Travelling People, but fear the political ramifications of being seen to do so, Best Value may offer an opportunity to make low-key and fair progress in this area. These ideas are by no means new:

> In considering the cost of provision for travellers, it is important that a local authority should attempt to add up all its previously hidden costs of coping with travellers in order to estimate the true cost of setting up a properly controlled site. Simply deducting the annual rent from the annual outgoings

on the site itself disguises the saving in time of a variety of officers and other employees of the authority, as well as of the police. Over and above these kinds of benefits, there will be the less tangible, but nonetheless real, effects on the community at large stemming from an improvement in amenity and reduced social friction, and on the travellers themselves as they begin to play a fuller part in community life. (Ministry of Housing and Local Government/ Welsh Office, 1967, p 68)

Notes

[1] Although devolved institutions such as the National Assembly of Wales and Scottish Parliament were effectively bound by the HRA provisions before then (see Clements, 1999).

[2] Also see www.cre.gov.uk/media/ for this 'Punch Retail' case, which established Irish Travellers to be such a group in Britain.

[3] In October 2000 European Union (EU) ministers agreed another Directive to combat discrimination in the workplace on grounds of age, sexual orientation, disability and religion or belief. The Employment Directive complements the EU Race Directive, and the combined force of the two Directives and the HRA will give individuals powerful legal rights to challenge discrimination, which could lead to more cases against local authorities.

SEVEN

Conclusion: obstacles and opportunities

It is worse than useless and unavailing to harass them from place to place when no retreat or shelter is provided. (Hoyland, 1816, p 161)

In 1992 the government proposed major reforms in the law relating to accommodation for Travelling People, implemented in 1994. The Labour government has retained the regime since coming into power in 1997; although a major review of housing law was commenced in 2000, no changes to policy relating to accommodation for Travelling People appear imminent.

A primary motive given for the 1994 reforms was financial: that the cost to the public purse of providing sites for Travelling People was unjustifiably high. Yet no study has ever looked into the costs of not providing sites. The availability and appropriateness of lawful stopping places is directly linked to the costs of 'unauthorised encampments', which costs have long been a matter of concern to a wide range of public and private organisations. A 1998 pilot survey by the Traveller Law Research Unit (TLRU) at Cardiff Law School indicated that the costs of non-provision might be at least as substantial as those of provision.

This book presents the findings of a subsequent and more comprehensive study by the TLRU of costs associated with unauthorised encampments. In addition to an exploration of financial costs experienced by UK local authorities, as landowners and providers of public services, it also examines financial, human and social costs suffered by private landowners and other settled people, police services and Travelling People themselves. The costs are placed in context by exploring both the 1992 process of legal change in this field, and obligations now placed on public bodies by 'Best Value' and other new laws.

Issues around and approaches to the costs of unauthorised encampments are perceptibly varied and complex, raising difficult and sometimes emotive questions. There has been no public debate on the costs of site provision compared to those of non-provision, and even less research. While concern about costs by local authorities is widespread, the reliable data available from authorities is patchy. It is evident that some public bodies would prefer this information not to be explicit, in order that they can continue to deal with encampments in an informal fashion; the issue being a political 'hot potato'. Unauthorised encampments are for the most part not yet considered, either locally or at national level, as an issue to which the Best Value regime – the pursuit of economy, efficiency and effectiveness – applies. The costs of such encampments are elusive but substantial.

Unauthorised encampments are usually a small issue on the scale of local authority and police business, yet issues around Travelling People are often raised by these bodies and by local media; they are a larger political 'issue' than their small population would suggest. For some authorities, encampments can be an ordeal; a respondent to the survey stated that dealing with encampments was a burden to it as a small authority with a high number of encampments. The data in Chapters Three and Four indicate that the costs of encampments in the UK are significant, in financial, human and social terms. The annual costs to local authorities alone run to many millions of pounds.

These costs are unlikely to reduce, as perceived by the high number of respondents to the TLRU study who believe costs to be static or rising. More traditional stopping places are being closed off each year, forcing nomadic Travelling People onto more highly visible and often less suitable locations; such encampments are likely to be more expensive than those that are 'tucked away', due to the level of disruption and dismay that can be complained of by settled people. Therefore more expenditure in one sector (the 'protection' of vulnerable sites) may result in yet more expenditure in other respects.

Considerable though the costs are, they can be hard to pin down. Many costs are easily measurable (although they are often not measured): legal costs such as court summonses and the hire of bailiffs; engineering and other measures to 'protect' land; officer time spent on sites, in transit, in meetings and on related paperwork. Other costs were identified by respondents as being difficult, if not impossible, to account for, particularly time spent dealing with complaints. Few respondent authorities stated concern about the costs experienced by Travelling People.

Even costs that are obvious and calculable are often concealed within departmental budgets. Therefore an unknown but considerable quantity of money is being expended each year on a matter that is a 'problem' for settled people twice over: unauthorised encampments are something that they do not wish to see but which they are continually paying for. By their failure to ensure accommodation provision for Travelling People as well as for 'settled', local and central government have effectively shifted the (relatively small) costs onto their populations in a form of (relatively higher) taxation. This does not appear to be 'money well spent', as the numbers of encampments and human, monetary and social costs associated with them continue to rise.

Recommendation 1: In keeping with Best Value principles, the obvious costs of unauthorised encampments should be accounted for by local authorities, police authorities and central government departments; less obvious costs to private landowners and Travelling People estimated; and local and national policies formally justified or amended by reference to them. This must be built into the Best Value audit regime through guidance from central government (perhaps via a national Best Value Performance Indicator).

The costs of unauthorised encampments might still be substantial, even if there were ample and ongoing provision of public sites for Travelling People. The example of the 1968 Caravan Sites Act regime indicates that such a programme would be slow to develop and show results, so that encampments would continue. Even if sites were to be built in appropriate locations and to a good standard of design and build, not all Travelling People would necessarily want to live on them. It is possible that there will always be some Travelling People who are highly mobile and create a large number of encampments, even if an extensive network of transit sites were to be built throughout the UK (just as there will always be homelessness regardless of the health of the housing market).

The costs of providing sites may be no less substantial than the costs of not doing so. Aside from the costs of land, design and construction, some people on sites will be dependent on housing and other benefits in order to meet the rent and other costs of 'settling down'. Therefore expenditure will still have to be made at local and national levels. However, these same issues exist in respect of 'settled' people, but are not used as justification to enable no housing provision.

As with housing, if people living on sites for whatever length of time felt safe and secure, that they had a 'stake' in where they live and that it was culturally appropriate for them, costs of non-provision would reduce over time. Well-designed and well-managed pitches on sites can be priced fairly and run without financial loss. The DTLR has commissioned research into the management, maintenance and provision of public sites, the results of which will not be published until 2002/03 and will not automatically lead to immediate policy development. More urgent action should be taken to ensure that local and national policies relating to accommodation for Travelling People are founded on facts and fairness, not intolerance and guesswork.

Recommendation 2: The relative virtues and problems associated with various policies on 'accommodating' Travelling People should be explicitly explored by central government and the costs and benefits properly assessed and weighed, in keeping with national policy programmes aimed at inclusion and equality of opportunity, such as *A decent home for all* (housing), *Bringing Britain together: a national strategy for neighbourhood renewal*, and *Opportunities for all* (enterprise, skills and innovation).

When the government proposed the repeal of the duty on local authorities to provide sites for Gypsies in 1992, one justification was that the cost of provision was too high a burden on the taxpayer. Not only did this wrongly suggest that Travelling People do not pay taxes, it did not take into account the potential costs of alternative policies.

The 1994 reforms were a cost-cutting exercise unencumbered by reference to detailed spreadsheets of projected savings in financial terms or social costs. Current policy in relation to stopping places (authorised or not) is founded on false premises; not justified by reference to objective and demonstrable indicators, nor to programmes promoting fairness and efficiency in public service provision for other sectors of society.

Essential components of Best Value are that local public bodies should base policies on hard data, and measure the impact of policies on such data in future. Central government has failed to analyse the costs associated with unauthorised encampments, to incorporate widespread cost concerns and considerations into policy development. This is not in keeping with the very Best Value, race relations and social inclusion principles it espouses.

As Travelling People have been moved on over the years, so the issues and problems related to their accommodation, or its lack, have also been moved on, by successive central governments and between different local bodies. It may be that the Best Value regime forces some local authorities or police (or both) to take 'ownership' of these issues. Or it may be that Travelling People, and costs associated with their 'stopping', will continue to be pushed back and forth without formal recognition or monitoring of the outcomes. If authorities and police services wait for the government to provide a clearer lead, they may in the meantime be taken to court by increasingly rights-aware Travelling People.

Recommendation 3: The impact on race and community relations of different approaches to unauthorised encampments and site provision, including a comparison with policy and provision for 'settled' people, should be undertaken by local public service providers and encompassed in the national survey at recommendation 2; in keeping with positive local and central government obligations under the race relations law to promote equality of opportunity and good race relations.

It is surely of concern that only one TLRU survey respondent cited Best Value in relation to unauthorised encampments, and that only a handful of authorities developing best practice in this area can currently be identified. Regardless of the policy that an authority adopts with respect to encampments, Best Value requires that it be formally reviewed, agreed and justified; race relations and human rights legislation that it be fair in application and effect.

Rather than treat Best Value, race relations and human rights obligations as a burden, they can be viewed as a boon. They provide public bodies with a combined set of tools to assist in working towards fair and effective service provision and public expenditure for all people living in an area, however briefly. Best Value and equality legislation offer authorities an opportunity to review the way in which they manage encampments, and to ensure that their policies and processes are both cost-effective and respectful of the rights and differences of settled and Travelling People alike.

References

ACERT (Advisory Council for the Education of Romany and other Travellers) and Wilson, M. (1997) *Directory of planning policies for Gypsy site provision in England*, Bristol: The Policy Press.

Adams, B., Okely, J., Morgan, D. and Smith, D. (1975) *Gypsies and government policy in England*, London: Heinemann.

Advisory Committee on Scotland's Travelling People (1978) *Second report*, Edinburgh: The Scottish Office Development Department.

Advisory Committee on Scotland's Travelling People (1998) *Eighth term report 1995-1997*, Edinburgh: The Scottish Office Development Department.

Advisory Committee on Scotland's Travelling People (1999) *Ninth term report 1998-1999*, Edinburgh: The Scottish Office Development Department.

Ansell, N. (1997) 'Travellers get their home sweet home', *The Big Issue*, 20-26 September.

Audit Commission (1998) *Better by far: Preparing for Best Value*, London: Audit Commission.

Audit Commission (1999) *Listen up! Effective community consultation*, at www.audit-commission.gov.uk/publications/best_value.shtml.

Audit Commission (2001a) *Another step forward*, London: Best Value Inspection Service of the Audit Commission.

Audit Commission (2001b) *Changing gear: Best Value annual statement 2001* (www.audit-commission.gov.uk).

Becker, H. (1963) *Outsiders: Studies in the sociology of deviance*, New York, NY: The Free Press of Glencoe, Macmillan Publishing Co, Inc.

Brighton and Hove Council (1999) *Draft Traveller strategy*, Brighton.

Bucke, T. and James, Z. (1998) *Trespass and protest: Policing under the Criminal Justice and Public Order Act 1994*, Home Office Research Study 190, London: Home Office.

Campbell, S. (1995) 'Gypsies: the criminalisation of a way of life?', *Criminal Law Review*, p 28.

Campbell, S. (1998) 'Eviction is a waste of money', *Housing*, vol 34, no 3, p 13.

Cardiff University School of Education (1998) *Traveller children and educational need in Wales*, Cardiff: Cardiff University/Save the Child Fund Wales Programme.

Cemlyn, S. (1998) *Policy and provision by social services for Traveller children and families,* Report on Research Study, Bristol: School for Policy Studies, University of Bristol.

Children's Participation Project (Wessex) (1998) *My dream site: Research with Traveller children around the issue of sites,* Bath: The Children's Society.

Clements, L. (1999) 'Devolution in Wales and the human rights implications', *Legal Action,* July, pp 20-1.

Clements, L. and Smith, P. (1997) *Traveller law reform: TLAST/TLRU conference and consultation report,* Cardiff: Traveller Law Research Unit, Cardiff Law School.

Connolly, P. and Keenan, M. (2000) *Racial attitudes and prejudice in Northern Ireland,* Belfast: Northern Ireland Statistics and Research Agency, Social Policy Branch.

Council of Europe (1995) *The situation of Gypsies (Roma and Sinti) in Europe,* Strasbourg: European Committee on Migration, CDMG (95)11, 5 May.

Cowan, D., Donson, F., Higate, F., Lomax, D. and Third, H. (2001) *The management of unauthorised camping: Monitoring the good practice guidance,* Research Paper No 77, Edinburgh: ECA School of Planning and Housing, Edinburgh College of Art/Heriot-Watt University.

Cowell, R., Martin, S. and MORI Local Government Unit (2001) *Joining up best value and other initiatives,* Report to the Improvement and Development Agency, Cardiff: Local and Regional Government Research Unit, Cardiff University/MORI.

CRE (Commission for Racial Equality) (1998) *Racial equality means quality,* revised version at www.cre.gov.uk/publs/cat-gov.html.

Cripps, J. (1976) *Accommodation for Gypsies: A report on the working of the Caravan Sites Act 1968,* London: HMSO, for the Department of the Environment and the Welsh Office.

Davis, J. (1997) 'New Age Travellers in the countryside', in P. Milbourne (ed) *Revealing rural 'others': Representation, power and identity in the British countryside,* London: Pinter.

Davis, J., Grant, R. and Locke, A. (1994) *Out of site, out of mind,* London: The Children's Society.

DETR (Department of the Environment, Transport and the Regions) (1998) *Improving services through Best Value,* London: DETR.

DETR (1999) Explanatory notes to the 1999 Local Government Act, London: The Stationery Office, available at www.official-documents.co.uk.

DETR (2000a) letter, 477/99/00 (24), 7 November.

DETR (2000b) *Quality and choice: A decent home for all*, Housing Green Paper, London: DETR.

DETR/Home Office (1998) *Managing unauthorised camping: A good practice guide*, London: DETR.

DoE (Department of the Environment) (1982) *The accommodation needs of long-distance and regional Travellers*, London: DoE (based on research carried out by D. Smith, G. Gmelch and S. Gmelch).

DoE and Welsh Office (1977) 'Gypsy Caravan Sites – Caravan Sites Act 1968 Part II', Circular 28 and 51/77.

DoE and Welsh Office (1978) 'Accommodation for Gypsies – Summary of and response for the Cripps Report', Circular 57/78 and 97/78.

DoE and Welsh Office (1994a) 'Gypsy sites and unauthorised camping', Circular 18/94 and 76/94, 23 November.

DoE and Welsh Office (1994b) 'Gypsy sites and planning', Circular 1/94 and 2/94.

Dorset County Council (1999) *Best Value proposal for environmental services*, Dorchester: Dorset County Council.

Dorset County Council Environmental Services Directorate (1999) *Managing unauthorised camping: Issues report*, Dorchester: Dorset County Council.

Duncan, A. (1999) Mr Alan Duncan, MP for Rutland and Melton, House of Commons debates for 10 May, col 88.

European Commission of Human Rights (1995) Application No 27238/95.

Geary, R. and O'Shea, C. (1995) 'Defining the travellers: from legal theory to practical action', *Journal of Social Welfare and Family Law*, vol 17, no 2, pp 167-78.

Green, H. and Office of Population Censuses and Surveys (1991) *Counting Gypsies*, London: HMSO.

Hawes, D. and Perez, B. (1996) *The Gypsy and the state: The ethnic cleansing of British society* (2nd edn), Bristol: The Policy Press.

HMIC (Her Majesty's Inspectorate of Constabulary) (1999) *Keeping the peace: Policing disorder*, London: Home Office.

HMIC (Her Majesty's Inspectorate of Constabulary) (2000) *Winning the race: Embracing diversity* (Consolidation Inspection of Police Community and Race Relations), London: Home Office.

Holtermann, S. (1998) *Weighing it up: Applying economic evaluations to social welfare programmes*, York: Joseph Rowntree Foundation.

Home Office (2000) *Core guidance for public authorities – a new era of rights and responsibilities* (Part 1), London (www.homeoffice.gov.uk).

Home Office Communication Directorate (2000) *Race equality in public services*, Annual Report, London: Home Office, available at www.homeoffice.gov.uk/new_indexs/index_racial-equality.htm.

Home Office Communication Directorate (2001) *Race equality in public services*, Annual Report, London: Home Office, available at www.homeoffice.gov.uk/new_indexs/index_racial-equality.htm.

Hoyland, J. (1816) *A historical survey of the customs, habits and present state of the Gypsies; designed to develop the origin of this singular people, and to promote the amelioration of their condition*, York: Hoyland.

Jones, T. and Newburn, T. (2001) *Widening access: Improving police relations with hard to reach groups*, Police Research Series Paper 138, London: Research, Development and Statistics Directorate, Home Office.

Joyce, D. (1999) 'Testimony', *European Roma Rights Centre newsletter, Roma Rights*, Budapest, no 3.

Kenrick, D. and Clark, C. (1999) *Moving on: The Gypsies and Travellers of Britain*, Hatfield: University of Hertfordshire Press.

Lambert, J. (1976) *Crime, police and race relations*, London: Oxford University Press.

LGAPC (Local Government Association Planning Committee) (1997) *Gypsy/Traveller issues*, Working Paper, 21 October, London: LGAPC.

Liberty (1995) *Criminalising diversity, criminalising dissent*, London: National Council for Civil Liberties.

Liégeois, J-P. (1987) *Gypsies and Travellers*, Strasbourg: Council of Europe.

Lloyd, L. (1993) 'Proposed reform of the 1968 Caravan Sites Act: producing a problem to suit a solution?', *Critical Social Policy*, vol 38, p 82.

London Borough of Hammersmith and Fulham (2001) *Equality in practice*, London: Commission for Racial Equality.

London Borough of Hillingdon and the Metropolitan Police (Hillingdon division) (1999) Protocol for Dealing with Unauthorised Encampments, March.

London Irish Women's Centre (1995) *Rights for Travellers: A survey of local authority provision for Travellers in London*, London.

MacPherson, W. (1999) *The Stephen Lawrence Inquiry Report*, Cmnd 4262, London: The Stationery Office.

Martin, S., Davis, H., Bovaird, T., Geddes, M., Hartley, J., Lewis, M., Sanderson, I. and Sapwell, P. (1999) *Improving local public services: Interim evaluation of the Best Value pilot programme*, London: DETR.

Mayall, D. (1995) *English Gypsies and state policies*, Hatfield: University of Hertfordshire Press.

Milton Keynes Council (1997) *Travellers and illegal encampments: Position statement*, November, p 22.

Milton Keynes Council (1999) *Report of Milton Keynes Citizens' Advisory Group on Travellers*, 24 March, p 20.

Ministry of Housing and Local Government/Welsh Office (1967) *Gypsies and other Travellers*, London: HMSO.

Morran, R., Lloyd, M., Carrick, K. and Barker, C. (1999) *Moving targets*, Edinburgh/Dundee: Save the Children/University of Dundee.

Morris, R. (1999) 'The invisibility of Gypsies and other Travellers', *Journal of Social Welfare and Family Law*, vol 21, no 4, pp 399-404.

Morris, R. (2000) 'Gypsies, Travellers and the media', *Tolley's Communications Law*, vol 5, no 6, pp 213-19.

Morris, R. and Clements, L. (eds) (1999) *Gaining ground: Law reform for Gypsies and Travellers*, Hatfield: University of Hertfordshire Press.

Morris, R. and Clements, L. (2001) *Disability, social care, health and Travelling People*, Cardiff: Traveller law Research Unit, Cardiff Law School.

Mulreany, M. (1991) 'Economy, efficiency and effectiveness in the public sector: key issues', in T. Hardiman and M. Mulreany, *Efficiency and effectiveness in the public domain*, Dublin: Irish Institute of Public Administration, pp 30-1.

Niner, P., Davis, H. and Walker, B. (1998) *Local authority powers for managing unauthorised camping*, London: DETR.

Northampton Borough Council (2001) *Best Value review of encampments report*, Northampton: Northampton Borough Council.

Northampton Police (2000) 'Travellers in Northamptonshire', Northampton: Northamptonshire Police.

OfSTED (Office for Standards in Education) (1996) *The education of travelling children*, London: Office of Her Majesty's Chief Inspector of Schools.

OfSTED (1998) *Raising the attainment of minority ethnic pupils*, London: Office of Her Majesty's Chief Inspector of Schools.

OfSTED (2001) *Managing support for the attainment of pupils from minority ethnic groups*, London: Office of Her Majesty's Chief Inspector of Schools.

OSCE (Organisation for Security and Co-operation in Europe) (2000) *Report on the situation of Roma and Sinti in the OSCE area*, The Hague (www.osce.org/ hcnm/documents/recommendations/roma/).

SCF (Save the Children Fund) (1998) *Failing the test*, Edinburgh.

Thomas, P. and Campbell, S. (1992) *Housing Gypsies*, Cardiff: Traveller Law Research Unit, Cardiff Law School.

Todd, D. and Clark, G. (1991) *Good practice guidelines for Gypsy site provision by local authorities*, London: DoE, HMSO.

Wealden District Council (2000) *Strategy for managing unauthorised camping*, Hailsham.

Webb, P. (1999) 'Summary of health and disability issues when working with the travelling community', MA Dissertation at the University of North London.

Webster, L. and Millar, J. (2001) 'The nature of employment for new travellers', Findings, for *Making a living: Social security, social exclusion and New Travellers*, Bristol/York: The Policy Press/Joseph Rowntree Foundation.

Williams, T. (1999) *Private Gypsy site provision*, Harlow: ACERT.

Appendix A: Further examples of concerns expressed by local authorities in relation to the costs of unauthorised encampments

Britain's first official site for [newer] travellers is now open but there's a catch – it's the only one. Travellers warn that Brighton and Hove Council may have created a merry-go-round with only one stop as the site has a six-month maximum stay.... In the council's innovative draft document, *Traveller Strategy*, council leader Lynette Gwyn-Jones says, "A never-ending chain of evictions has cost our country vastly more in legal and other costs than a solution based in site-provision and temporary stopping places would have". Gwyn-Jones' election to leader is a marked shift from the policies of her predecessor, Labour peer Lord Bassam, who once remarked that travellers should be "driven out of town". In the five year period from 1992-97 there were 300 evictions in East Sussex, 70 of them in Brighton and Hove. Nationally, the cost of evicting travellers has been estimated at £10-35 million every year. (Ansell, 1997, p 5)

The strategy document referred to also states that:

The mismatch of numbers of Travellers within the Sussex area and numbers of sites on which they can legally stay has inevitably led to high numbers of evictions. Throughout East Sussex alone there were an estimated 300 evictions in the five year period from 1992 to 1997 of which around 70 were in Brighton and Hove. Although no attempt has been made to quantify the legal and other costs associated with those evictions the costs of each one will vary from a few hundred pounds to several thousand representing a huge expenditure of resources on the process of chasing Travellers from one site to another. (Brighton and Hove Council, 1999, p 7)

The County of Avon was asked by a local Traveller support group in 1994 how much it had spent on unauthorised encampments; in correspondence it estimated that in 1993/94 the costs of facilities and evictions together had been £239,874. It also stated that:

... there will be a proportion of the time spent by Central Support Departments on travellers generally which is not broken down into further detail and therefore it is difficult to quantify. If you were to assume, for the sake of argument, that 50% of this was spent on evictions and related issues this would amount to a further £221,000.

In addition, an estimated 70% of the Travellers Co-ordination Unit's time is probably spent on unauthorised encampments and related matters. This would equate to approximately £101,500. Highways estimate a figure of £33,000. Community Resources estimate a figure of £4,000.

Education estimate a total of £33,000 for transport costs and make the point that this figure has been reduced to £2,990 so far this year due to the opening of the Winterbourne and Ashfield Farm site and a lesser number of evictions concerning school children. The Service is not able to differentiate its costs between children on official sites and off sites however it is suggested that the costs are higher off sites.

On a rough calculation based on the above it might be said that the cost of unauthorised encampments to the County Council is in the order of £632,374. However, in addition to the above, you will be aware that there have been settlements with aggrieved landowners which may run close to a further £100,000. In contrast … the official sites are meant to be self-financing or showing a surplus and in general they are.

Within Avon, Bristol City Council alone estimated, in correspondence with TLAST, that it had spent nearly £250,000 in 1996/97 and nearly £200,000 the following year, not including the revenue costs of professional input from departments and directorates (the value of which was estimated at £100,000 per annum in terms of diverted human resources). It also estimated that, if sites were not built to accommodate Travelling People in the area, securing site boundaries to avoid 'unwanted incursion' would exceed £1 million and impede the access onto these pieces of land for all city residents. The costs of clearing up after and providing services to Travelling People was estimated by the City Council to be about £200,000 a year.

In March 1999 the Milton Keynes Citizens' Advisory Group produced a report resulting from 1,200 hours of meetings, consultations and deliberations. The report described the process developed for the consultation with 'stakeholders' and set out the key findings. These included that the annual cost of dealing with unauthorised encampments – including preventative measures, cleaning up operations and repairs – was estimated at £360,000.

A London Borough estimated that unauthorised encampments had cost it £10,000 over 11 months:

The costs have been incurred during a period in which the Travellers have usually been moved on as quickly as was reasonably practicable. There is no provision, within existing budgets, to adopt a more proactive approach to the problem of illegal encampments.... Members are asked to endorse the view that there are no sites within Ealing that are suitable as transit sites for Travellers and that the policy must therefore be to discourage unauthorised encampments; to evict Travellers from them, and to do so as quickly as possible using all appropriate means ... the frequency and duration of unauthorised encampments during the past year has resulted in significant additional work.... (London Borough of Ealing internal minutes, 1996, paragraphs 3 and 10.3)

One County Council's costs for eviction from only two locations in 1997 were over £22,000. The costs estimated by them over the same period for site provision over a six-month adjusted period were £11,240 (excluding land costs but including establishment and management).

According to research by the Children's Society, the cost of providing small transit sites "must appear better 'value for money' than the costs of enforcing evictions; housing travellers who become homeless; offering increased benefit payments (such as housing benefit); and meeting the additional costs of policing travellers" (Davis et al, 1994, p 14).

A Local Government Association Planning Committee working paper (LGAPC, 1997) states the following:

> With large-scale incursions, it is widely accepted that the 1994 Act powers are virtually unworkable. This has been the experience at the Crowborough site in Wealden District, where a large encampment has been in situ since January 1995. The costs of attempted eviction are around £170,000. In the case of other authorities over the last year or so, they are: Tewkesbury £250,000 and Doncaster £100,000. Many other authorities around the country have smaller enforcement costs, but these are nevertheless a drain on resources. (paragraph 6)

The same document also acknowledges the costs of unauthorised encampments to Travellers:

> The present situation where gypsies/travellers are, in effect, caught in a vicious circle where there are not enough pitches on local authority run sites, not enough private pitches, and they are continually moved on from other unauthorised sites, is clearly unsatisfactory. Occupying unsuitable sites where proper facilities, eg drinking water, sanitation, do not exist is unsatisfactory in terms of health and general well-being. Continually moving from short-term site to short-term site disrupts the education of travellers' children. The whole process increases social alienation among travellers and, particularly where sensitive sites are concerned near residential areas, increases the traditional hostility on the part of the settled population to those pursuing a nomadic lifestyle. There are clearly, therefore,

implications for other service areas, eg Education, Social Services and Housing....
(paragraph 8)

In March 1998 a Gloucestershire school admitted a handful of Traveller children who
had recently arrived in the area. Almost immediately, more than 100 children from the
local settled community were removed by their parents in protest. One resulting
letter to the local newspaper stated:

For children of both groups it will be a lesson in intolerance, teaching the majority
it is alright to exclude a minority, teaching the minority that they cannot expect
justice ... the present situation has arisen in part because the travellers are camping
near the school on land to which they have no right.... The local authority reaction,
here as elsewhere, is to do nothing constructive, leaving difficulties to reach such
a peak that hostilities become inevitable, leading to the use of court orders which
force them elsewhere. The problem, however, does not go away, it goes round and
round. (*The Citizen*, 26 March 1998, p 11)

According to an English District Council:

The economic, social and environmental impacts of [Travellers'] presence have
been numerous and much anecdotal evidence of this has been received. There are
also real and quantifiable costs involved in limiting and controlling illegal occupation
of land and less obvious but equally significant cost in terms of the interruption to
planned work and the delay in responding to other important issues and priorities
as a result ... there will always be a need for a reactive response to occupation, but
this year has shown the considerable costs involved in that. A proactive response
based on securing our sites better could in the long-run save resources and
considerably reduce the impact on a wide range of service areas mounting responses
to illegal occupation when it occurs. (Arun District Council, Policy & Resources
Committee, 15 September 1999, Agenda Item No 16)

The Council paper goes on to state the need to protect a number of potential sites
from encampments by the provision of 'knee rails' around the perimeter and gates, at
an estimated cost of £42,563.

Appendix B: 1998 TLRU pilot study on the costs of unauthorised encampments

Sue Campbell, TLAST Advice Worker, Traveller Law Research Unit

These findings were first published, in a different format, in *Housing* magazine (Campbell, 1998, p 13).

This is a preliminary analysis and report prepared from a Telephone Legal Advice Service for Travellers (TLAST, part of the Traveller Law Research Unit at Cardiff Law School 1995-98) survey and research during 1998 on the financial cost of unauthorised encampments borne by local authorities. Last June TLAST contacted all metropolitan borough councils (MBCs), London borough councils (LBCs), new unitary authorities (UAs) and county councils (CCs) in England and Wales to seek their participation in the research. So far 78 responses have been received – a 55% response rate. District councils (DCs) have not been included in the survey at this stage.

Never before has such a nationwide survey been conducted; this is surprising, because as long ago as 1976 the Cripps Report (*Accommodation for Gypsies*) highlighted the vast amount of time and money spent on evictions and preventative measures to deter further encampments. Sir John Cripps cited one MBC as having spent £18,000 (in 1975-76 prices) and concluded that the provision of sites would result in savings for local authorities.

A recent report of the Local Government Association's planning committee puts the attempted eviction costs at Crowborough at £170,000 and notes that £100,000 was spent by Doncaster in similar eviction action. Todd and Clark (1991) in *Good practice guidelines for Gypsy site provision by local authorities*, quoted one LBC as having spent £120,000 on site protection and clearing rubbish alone. A report to the housing committee of Canterbury City Council on 21 October 1992 states that £24,138 was spent on 38 cases, although £6,400 of this sum was recovered from private landowners after the council took action on their behalf. One city council informed the DoE that it spent £71,000 in 1990 on evictions from illegal transit camps (Parliamentary Debates [*Hansard*], 10 February 1994).

What is clear from the preliminary analysis of the survey responses is that only one local authority appears to have calculated the total cost, while the remaining authorities have excluded one or more items from their calculations. Typically, the sort of costs councils are likely to incur are legal costs including court fees and attendance, counsels' fees, costs for solicitors' time, bailiffs' fees and hire of removal vehicles where necessary. Social services, housing, education, environmental services and planning departments are also likely to have substantial costs for site visiting, preparing reports on Travellers' needs, and interdepartmental liaison; the costs of staff time for such work is a major factor. Substantial sums are spent clearing and cleaning sites after eviction and securing the site against further illegal occupation by fencing, trenching and other measures to ensure that a site is inaccessible. An estimation of the cost of police time has not been included in any authority's calculations.

Of the 28 (out of 35) CCs that responded, three declared they had no costs. One stated that its only eviction cost was a token payment to a parish council, yet it was very obvious from its policy and practice guidelines that unauthorised encampments did occur but tended to be resolved by discussion and dialogue with the Traveller groups concerned – all consuming officer time (and therefore costly activities). This particular CC employed a full-time Traveller Liaison Officer, yet no account had been taken of the attendant salary costs. Salaries for Gypsy Liaison Officers vary from one authority to another but are likely to be between £16,000 and £25,000 net. The same applies to the two other CCs, which reported no costs but employed Traveller Liaison Officers.

Seven CCs were unable to provide any information on costs at all, but from the information given it was clear that significant sums were involved and that the majority employed Gypsy Liaison Officers. A majority of these CCs registered high Gypsy counts, and arguably an analysis of such cost would be essential information.

Twelve out of the 28 CCs that responded were able to provide a 'guesstimate' of total costs; these ranged from £8,000 to £30,000 per annum, with an average of £20,450, but the majority had made no provision for the cost of staff time. Neither did the calculations of eight of these authorities include the cost of building works or site clearing in their totals. In total, a sum of £245,400 was spent by these 12 CCs, but only four had included building works and site clearance (to the tune of £64,200) in their total costs. Substantial additional amounts are likely to have been spent on site clearance. Only five CCs have arrived at a figure per eviction: this averaged £1,080.

As for CCs' legal costs, only eight were able to provide any figures (average £5,200), the lowest being £1,000, with two putting their costs at £10,000 each. In total, a sum of £42,350 was spent but only one had included staff time.

Of 27 UAs in England, only nine responded. Three of these could not state what their costs were and three other UAs stated that no costs were involved. No UA could provide a total cost. However, one UA did spend in excess of £10,000 in pursuit of a single eviction through the courts, although only £170 of that sum was in respect of legal fees, which excluded officer time. Another UA estimated the cost of eviction per site at around £5,000, inclusive of legal fees and clearing the site after eviction.

Out of 36 MBCs, 13 responses were received; of these, nine were able to provide a total cost figure. Only one MBC was unable to quantify cost because it claimed not to have a significant problem with unauthorised encampments. No MBC stated it had no costs at all. The total figure for these 13 authorities adds up to £152,580. Two MBCs recorded costs in excess of £50,000 each.

One MBC referred to a high level of unauthorised encampments, and spent a total of £70,000 including officer time and site clearance, £30,000 of which was spent on fencing to prevent further encroachments. This authority has only recently appointed a Travellers' Officer.

Another MBC recorded a budget of £52,000 used to clear up and secure sites after unauthorised encampments; this sum excludes officer time and suggests that the reduced number of unauthorised encampments is attributed to the improved security of its land. The lowest total annual cost quoted is £420, which that MBC attributes to its policy of toleration and a reduction in the number of Travellers 'stopping off' in its area. Only three MBCs were able to provide a figure in respect of legal costs, with an average legal cost per eviction of £324.

Fourteen (out of 33) LBCs responded to the survey; three stated no costs were involved because successful policies of negotiation eliminated the need for proceedings. This again suggests that generally the cost of unauthorised encampments is only quantified if it involves actual out-of-pocket expenditure. Another five LBCs could not say what their costs were, the majority stating that in any event there had been no illegal encampments. Only three LBCs were able to provide a total cost figure: one spent £30,000 on three encampments and appears to have taken all likely costs into account.

One LBC reported two large eviction actions, of which the most expensive ran up legal costs of £5,000, excluding the cost of the borough's solicitors' time. Another LBC established a 'task force' of officers from social services, education and housing departments who visit the site and report on Travellers' needs at a cost of £300-400 per incident, with legal costs of £320, and vehicle hire between £100 and £200. This LBC estimates a sum in excess of £1,000 for an encampment on a small scale.

Twelve out of a possible 22 UAs in Wales responded, four declaring no incidents of unauthorised encampments and therefore no cost. Seven UAs provided a total cost, averaging £1,810 per annum. Of those UAs that responded, the preliminary findings indicate that, overall, Welsh local authorities report fewer incidences of unauthorised encampments compared with English authorities. Only one UA had made a calculation of the legal costs involved.

A total of £454,655 was spent by those local authorities that responded to our survey. If an average figure is taken for each type of local authority surveyed, based on the information supplied by survey respondents, and if that figure is then multiplied by the total number of local authorities, we can estimate that £2,009,905 represents total eviction costs borne by local authorities in England and Wales in 1997-98, an amount that in the vast majority of cases takes no account of staff time or building works. If the same computation is applied to legal costs, we can estimate an additional total figure of £438,131.

An annual figure of £2,448,036 is almost certainly a substantial underestimate. Almost without exception, the local authorities that provided estimates of their costs failed to take into account (or to fully account for) staff time. Most local authorities have also failed to include the substantial costs of site clearance and the engineering and/or building works to secure the land against re-entry.

Those local authorities that have taken some or all of these factors into account record significantly higher costs (in the order of at least 100% higher).

Even if we assumed only a 50% error, this would result in the annual cost to local authorities being in the order of over £3.5 million. The final research report will endeavour to quantify the probable cost with greater precision and confidence. However, these preliminary calculations take no account of the cost of police involvement in either civil or criminal evictions; this is likely to be substantial.

Likewise, the preliminary estimate takes no account of expenditure made by DCs because in the first phase of this research project we did not survey DC costs. Some DCs face extremely high costs, such as Wealden District Council (in relation to the Crowborough eviction) and Canterbury City Council. In one (unsolicited) return, a DC recorded that £1,200 per eviction was spent; this sum was apportioned equally between legal costs and physical enforcement costs. The DC averaged 16 evictions per year, giving an annual cost of £19,200. If this figure were typical (and there is no evidence either way), it would mean that the 260 DCs faced a total cost of £4,992,000 per annum.

At this stage of the research, it is too early to predict the likely total cost of 'non-site' provision to public authorities. However, it is probably safe to assume that the 'conservative' estimated costs of £3.5 million for CCs, MBCs, LBs and UAs would be at least doubled if the estimated costs borne by DCs and police were included.

Of course, these figures include neither eviction action taken by individual private landowners, nor evictions in respect of enforcement action by planning authorities. Nor are the eviction costs of other large land-owning bodies included (such as the National Trust, Railtrack, water authorities and so on) or of government departments and agencies (such as the Ministry of Defence, Department of Employment, Department of Trade and so on); these costs are likely to be considerable.

In a recent parliamentary debate (House of Commons [*Hansard*], 16 July 1997), the issue of the cost of evictions from unauthorised encampments was raised, when Mr Edward Garnier MP (Harborough) spoke of an illegal encampment in his constituency. He said that "a vast amount of public money had been spent dealing with the encampment – not just on police and local authority officers' time, but on lawyers' fees, legal aid, home office inquiries by me, and the collective dealing with the public inquiries by the several agencies involved".

One of the reasons given for abolishing the duty on local authorities to provide sites was a concern to cut public expenditure. The previous government stated in its August 1992 consultation paper that the cost of site provision over a period of 14 years had been £56 million (that is, £4 million per annum). The preliminary findings of this research project would suggest that the financial cost of not providing sites may be no less significant.

Appendix C: 1999 TLRU questions to local authorities on the costs to them of unauthorised encampments

1) Has your authority had to spend anything in connection with any unauthorised encampments of Gypsies or Travellers during the year between 1 September 1998 and 31 August 1999? YES/NO
   If so, please state how many encampments, and how many Travellers (put 'E' if estimate).

2) Is there a budget for some or all of this activity? How much is it, and who manages it?

3) Does your authority record the financial costs it bears in responding to these encampments? YES/NO

4) If the answer to question 3 was 'yes', please provide details of these costs in the table overleaf [see Table 3.1, page 42].
   If your answer was 'no', do you feel able to provide a 'guesstimate' of the costs to your authority of responding to unauthorised encampments? If so, please complete the table overleaf as well as you are able.

5) Does your authority employ a Gypsy/Traveller Liaison Officer? YES/NO
   If so, would your authority employ such an officer if there were significantly fewer (or no) unauthorised encampments in your area? YES/NO

6) What percentage of the cost of responding to unauthorised encampments would you estimate is in respect of Travellers with local connections, and with those Travellers who could be termed 'long-distance'? (By 'long distance' we mean Travellers who come to your area only once or twice a year and often only remain for relatively short periods).

7) Do you believe that the annual cost to your authority of responding to unauthorised encampments is increasing or decreasing in real terms? INCREASING/DECREASING
   Please briefly state your reasons for this belief.

8) Do you have any other comments on the issue of the costs of responding to unauthorised encampments?

Appendix D: 1992 consultation paper on reform of the 1968 Caravan Sites Act, and excerpts of some responses to the consultation

On 18 August 1992, the Homelessness Policy Division of the Department of the Environment issued a letter in which comments were invited on an enclosed consultation paper by 13 November 1992. A separate but parallel consultation was simultaneously undertaken in Wales by the Welsh Office.

The paper was stated in the letter to contain:

> ... proposals for reform in relation to the use of land by gypsies and other travellers in England and Wales. (As the paper says, the proposals are not directed at travelling showpeople.) The proposals in the enclosed paper entail improved powers for local authorities to move from land all illegal campers; encouraging gypsies and other travellers to move into more permanent housing; and putting gypsies on an equal footing within the planning system with anyone else who needs planning permission.

The letter added that: "Paragraph 25 of the enclosed paper refers to Ministers' intention that Exchequer grant to cover the capital costs of providing gypsy caravan sites should cease to be payable generally. I am writing separately today to every local authority in England to set out the factors which the Secretary of State will take into account in considering future applications for grant from authorities".

What follows is the text of the consultation paper, and some of the responses to it. The text of the paper is in normal print, whereas some of the comments sent to the government during the consultation period have been interspersed and are given in boxes with author name(s) in brackets. Some of the formatting of the consultation paper has been changed to avoid confusion, but the text remains exactly as in the original:

Reform of the 1968 Caravan Sites Act

1 The Conservative Manifesto 1992 noted that illegal camping by gypsies and other travellers could affect the lives of whole communities. It contained an undertaking to review the Caravan Sites Act 1968 with the aim of reducing the nuisance of illegal encampments. This consultation paper invites views on the Government's proposals for reform.

The Conservatives 1992 election manifesto gave an undertaking to review the 1968 Caravan Sites Act with the aim of reducing the nuisance of illegal encampments. However, the proposals they are instead putting forward will undoubtedly increase the number of Travellers forced to camp illegally. (Liberty [National Council for Civil Liberties])

The fact that the Government has recognised the problems being caused by unlawful or illegal campers and are considering changes in the law is to be welcomed. However the proposals themselves need to be considered carefully both in relation to the social problems which they could cause and the costs which could fall on local authorities. (Association of District Secretaries)

Purpose of the 1968 Act

2　In 1966 the then Minister of Housing commented that "... the remarkable fact (is) that for most traveller families there is nowhere they can put their homes; they are within the law only when moving along the road...". In 1965, there were estimated to be some 3,400 gypsy families (or about 4,750 caravans) in England and Wales, only a tiny fraction of whom were on authorised sites.

The 1965 statistics which revealed some 3,400 gypsy caravans was not based on accurate statistical surveys. It is also considered that the present count of caravans is probably not accurate. Local authorities vary in their approach to the counting of gypsy caravans present in their areas and it is understood that some authorities will make a nil return rather than accept the fact that they are presently required to make provision for gypsy caravans sites. (Canterbury City Council)

The practical result of the proposals, if implemented, would probably be a return to the conditions which led to the introduction of the 1968 Act – the existence of a footloose gypsy population, with nowhere that they could legally go, perpetually chased from place to place by local authorities in response to complaints from local residents. There would also be severe dissatisfaction on the part of authorities which had already achieved designation, who would see their hard-earned advantages swept away by the universal availability of the new legal remedies. (Association of County Councils)

3　In order to meet the needs of these travellers Parliament passed the Caravan Sites Act in 1968. This Act places on local authorities (County, Metropolitan District and London Borough Councils) a duty to accommodate all those whom the Act defined as "persons of nomadic habit of life, whatever their race or origin" and who were "residing in or resorting to their area".

4 To ensure there would be enough pitches not only for the travellers belonging to the area, but for those who travelled through it from time to time, the Act provided for "the establishment of ... (caravan) sites by local authorities for the use of gypsies and other persons of nomadic habit and (to) control in certain areas the unauthorised occupation of land by such persons".

> [T]here are families who want to go into a house (from sites, from the roadside) and have been on the Housing List for a decade or more without success. The main reason given is the shortage of housing! There are difficulties meeting the criteria, one of which is to have local connections. (The Green Paper's suggestion of banning illegal campers from an area for two years is going to make this process totally impossible.) (Cardiff Gypsy Sites Group)

5 Once a local authority was deemed to have provided sufficient pitches it could apply to become "designated" by the Secretary of State. The effect of designation is that it becomes a criminal offence for any gypsy to station a caravan for the purpose of residing within the designated area for any period on any land situated within the boundaries of a highway, or any other unoccupied land, or any occupied land without the consent of the landowner or tenant.

6 In this way it was intended that there should be sufficient provision of pitches for all travellers across the country, and that each local authority and area would accept a fair share of travellers. The intention was "... with this legislation and the provision of permanent camps the task of integration should become much easier ...".

Need for reform

7 Eric Lubbock, the then MP who introduced the Caravan Sites Bill, expected that it would "... help local authorities control the unauthorised use of land. It would give relief to quiet neighbourhoods and beautiful countryside which has suffered from invasions of the travelling people while at the same time it would give those travelling people a recognised place in the community ...".

8 The problem has grown faster than its remedy. Whereas in 1965 there were thought to be some 3,400 gypsy caravans, in January 1992 local authorities counted nearly 13,500 such caravans (an estimated 9,900 families) in England and Wales. Of these, over 4,500 were on unauthorised sites, only 1% fewer than in 1981. Only 38% of English local authorities have achieved designation in the 24 years that have elapsed since the Caravan Sites Act – despite the

fact that since 1978 a 100% grant has been available to meet the capital costs of gypsy sites, which so far has cost the Exchequer some £56 million.

> The Cripps Report draws attention to the very substantial public subsidy of housing; through local government public housing for rent. In addition the housing sector receives very substantial subsidy through the Housing Corporation and by mortgage interest relief; gypsies provide their own caravans and receive no public subsidy whatsoever in the purchase of their home; their caravan. They receive no interest relief and no Income Support assistance with the purchase cost repayments. The cost to the Exchequer of £56 million (over a 14 year period) referred to at paragraph 8 of the consultation paper is in this context extremely small. (Thorpes Solicitors, Hereford)

9 There are now nearly 9,000 gypsy caravans on authorised sites in England and Wales. But site provision is not keeping pace with the growth in the number of caravans, and the Government considers there is no reason why this need should automatically be met by public provision, nor any reason why gypsies – once settled – should remain on public sites indefinitely. The 1968 Act was intended to provide a network of sites to enable gypsies to move around or settle but in practice many gypsies have settled on permanent sites and 90% of local authority pitches in England are used for residential as opposed to transit purposes.

> There's definitely a need for more sites. They forget that as Travellers have kids and grow up and have their families, there's nowhere for them to go. That's why lots of Travellers are being forced into houses. All of Johnny's family and all of mine are now living in houses. (Nellie Power, Traveller, in London Irish Women's Centre, 1995, p 17)

10 At the time of the introduction of the Caravan Sites Act, it was observed that "… gypsies no longer follow the traditional occupations of many years ago such as horse dealing, handicrafts and fortune telling … more than half of them deal in scrap metal and particularly in car breaking …". In addition, many gypsies used to be regularly employed as temporary labour for farmers, who were content to let them camp on their land during, for example, the fruit-picking season.

11 Today, whilst the mechanisation of agriculture has lessened the scope for travellers to carry out fruit picking and other related activities, many travellers still earn a living from activities which require little start-up investment and can be pursued outdoors such as scrap metal dealing. There is less need to move from place to place, although conversely motor vehicles have enhanced travellers' mobility in comparison with the days of the horse-drawn van. So, while some traveller families retain a yearning to travel the open road,

many have settled on permanent sites and a few have moved into permanent housing.

> It is wrong to suggest that the Gypsy economy is made up only of outdated trades and occupations. Gypsies are capable of adapting their skills to meet new needs as they have always done. Seasonal and intermittent economic opportunities still mean that Gypsies need to travel to make their substantial contribution to the British economy. (The Gypsy Council for Education, Culture, Welfare and Civil Rights)

12 The situation has become more complex in recent years with the emergence of groups who do not wish to use sites that are provided, may travel in large numbers, may not be nomadic, and for whom the 1968 Act provisions may not have been designed. These may include some of the group colloquially known as New Age Travellers as well as the highly mobile families (identified in a 1965 gypsy study by the Ministry of Housing) who travel widely earning their living by laying tarmacadam. The Government considers that for the 1990s a fresh policy is needed which recognises the considerably greater number of travellers and the lessons which have been learned over the last 25 years.

> We do not understand what is meant by "the emergence of persons who travel in large numbers who may not be nomadic". Surely this statement is contradictory? (The Gypsy Council for Education, Culture, Welfare and Civil Rights)

> There are inconsistencies within the paper which make its purpose difficult to discern. It seems to have been written in a vacuum without reference to the stream of well-researched information which has been initiated by or is available to the government's own department in various reports, recommendations and guidelines. (Religious Society of Friends, Quaker Social Responsibility and Education)

> [W]e consider that the present problems have arisen simply because the numbers of true Romany stock who can perhaps be regarded as the only genuine "gipsies" are vastly outnumbered by imitators and persons who are unhappy to live within the social system. This is why we consider that the Romany Union should be invited to assist in sorting out the wheat from the chaff. (Harbledown Parish Council)

> The proposals for the pursuance of criminal proceedings against travellers will place a burden on local authorities with no benefit to society and, indeed, is likely to result in greater public order problems and increased homelessness. The enforcement penalties against travellers are seen by all member authorities to be unworkable, impractical and expensive, placing an unacceptable burden on local authorities in terms of housing and social services provision ... some of our member authorities have suggested that

the phenomenon of "new age travellers" is due to Government proposals emphasising market rents and withdrawal of access to finance for local authorities which have excluded many people from access to affordable and available housing. (Association of Metropolitan Authorities)

The problem

13 Camping causes particular concern when travellers

a) camp unlawfully [without authorisation and remediable under civil law] on someone else's land without their permission, which is only illegal [an offence usually covered by criminal law] and an offence in designated areas (see paragraph 5 above); or

b) camp on someone else's land with their permission but unlawfully because in breach of planning controls; or

c) camp and commit an offence, for example aggravated trespass or persistent nuisance.

Nothing in the paper recognises the deprivation and victimisation of gipsies and the racism which lies behind it. Nor is the extent to which present problems result from judicially established failure of local authorities to obey the law even mentioned. (Liberal Democrat Lawyers)

14 A number of powers are available to deal with illegal and unlawful camping. Their effectiveness and use vary. Where camping involves an offence the 1968 Act (paragraph 15), the Public Order Act 1986 (paragraph 16) and the Environmental Protection Act 1990 (paragraph 19) will be relevant. Where the camping is unlawful, civil law (paragraph 17) or the Planning and Compensation Act 1991 (paragraph 20) would make some camping unlawful in future, but no change is proposed in respect of breaches of planning controls.

[M]any of the current difficulties with site provision, unlawful camping and evictions are caused by the erosion of rights of access to traditional sites and stopping places. Since the Second World War a combination of social, economic and, above all, legislative change has deprived Gypsies and Travellers of the traditional sites and patterns of encampment they previously enjoyed. Legislative developments over the past 35 years have created extensive powers of prohibition and eviction. (Save the Children Fund)

The 1968 Caravan Sites Act

15 As explained above (paragraph 5), this Act enables the Secretary of State to designate local authorities who have made adequate provision for sites in their area or which he considers need not do so. An authority which is designated has access to fast-acting powers through a Magistrates' Court to remove unlawfully parked caravans and their occupants from highway land, unoccupied land or occupied land with the consent of the owner. However, these powers are limited because:

a) they are only available against Gypsies, defined in the Caravan Sites Act as "persons of nomadic habit of life, whatever their race or origin";

b) they are not available where the landlord or tenant consents to the illegal encampment even though intolerable nuisance may be caused to the surrounding community; and

c) by definition, they are not available to the 62% of local authorities which are not yet designated.

> The tone and the content of the Paper suggests that Gypsy sites and illegal encampments are a nuisance. It clearly attempts to give credence to the prejudices common among the public at large and landowners, by putting their interests above the interests of Gypsies. There is no recognition in the Paper of Gypsies as a distinct ethnic group (as established by CRE v Dutton (1989)) with a culture and a lifestyle that does not fit within the concept of static housing. Many Gypsies find it impossible to imagine living in a house for a variety of reasons – for example the cultural taboo against inside toilets. This is not a "choice" as the Paper implies, but a cultural necessity. (Cardiff City Council)

The 1986 Public Order Act

16 Section 39 of the 1986 Act enables the Police to act where aggravated trespass on land occurs. The effectiveness of these powers may be limited because:

a) they are only available where aggravated trespass has occurred and are used at the discretion of the senior police officer;

b) trespass may be on unoccupied or highway land not covered by Section 39 of the Act; and

c) it is a criminal offence to return to the same land as a trespasser but only for three months after a direction to leave the site has been given by the senior police officer present when aggravated trespass occurred.

> The current situation whereby travellers can obtain special unemployment benefit or income support: if the rules appertaining to the payment of such benefits were to be reviewed, we feel that the movement of such groups would be curtailed, thereby bringing about an element of encouragement to settle. (Police Federation of England and Wales)

> Similar situations to the above scenario have been experienced in Camden, where the provisions of S.39 of the Public Order Act were used to move Travellers. This has shown that local authority resources will be overstretched, especially if such situations arise over and over again. This is apart from the cost in terms of human misery to the children and families involved. (London Borough of Camden)

Civil remedies

17 A landowner whose land is *not* in a designated area and who is aggrieved by unlawful camping can only seek redress by initiating a civil action at his own expense. Landowners can apply to the court for an order of possession if they believe their property is unlawfully occupied, and special procedures are available through both the High Court and the county court to assist landowners in obtaining relief as quickly as possible. But many landowners may find that these procedures consume time and money and, if the campers return later or simply camp again nearby, they may be ineffective.

> Where the landowner faces illegal encampment whether it be by a gypsy or a new age traveller, he will normally face the costs of obtaining a possession order. Whether the encampment is by a small or large number he will usually face problems of cleaning up the land once the order is enforced. There are often delays between when the order is obtained and when it is enforced. Where trespass takes place there is usually some form of intimidation and at the very least the landowner is between £1,000-£2,000 out of pocket.... Landowners, therefore, bear the brunt of the costs of mass trespass and they have no real means of obtaining or recouping their expenditure. (Country Landowners Association)

Powers against breaches of planning controls

18 If there is unauthorised use of private land as a residential caravan site, the local planning authority may take planning enforcement action to remedy the breach of planning control either against gypsies who own or lease the land or against the landowner who has permitted the unauthorised use. The Planning and Compensation Act 1991 has provided greatly strengthened planning enforcement powers to remedy any breach of planning control. In particular, improved "stop notice" provisions now enable the local planning authority for the first time to prohibit the use of land as a residential caravan site, if necessary immediately. And there is provision for a new type of injunction to be sought against any actual or apprehended breach of control, even where the identity of the person allegedly responsible for the breach is unknown. It will be some time before the overall effect of these improvements can be properly assessed.

[T]he planning system should apply equally to gypsies and travellers providing it is responsive to the non-conventional residential demands which are placed on land by the travelling community. There are already precedents for this in the way the planning system deals with agricultural workers, the elderly and the infirm. (Council for the Protection of Rural England)

The 1990 Environmental Protection Act

19 Where a landowner is absent, or unknown, or allows the use of his land by travellers, but neighbours object on the ground that the camping creates a nuisance which requires immediate remedy, there should be scope for action under the Environmental Protection Act 1990. It is for the local authority to decide whether a particular activity amounts to a statutory nuisance under the 1990 Act, and whether to serve a notice on the person who causes the nuisance requiring remedial action, for example the cessation of noise or clearing up accumulations of rubbish. Breach of such a notice is an offence, incurring a fine.

Whilst we accept that the situation on and around unauthorised Gypsy sites can and invariably does lead to rubbish being accumulated, in the majority of cases the blame lies not with the family or families using the land as a campsite, but with the individual Local Authorities who are anxious not to be seen condoning such unauthorised camping by providing skips or plastic refuse sacks ... no decent Gypsy actually wants to live with the filth and squalor associated with unauthorised sites. (National Gypsy Council)

The government's proposals to tackle illegal camping

20 Unlawful or illegal campers who may invade land may cause much damage and distress to the landowner (or an occupier such as a tenant farmer) and/or to local people. The Government considers that the existing powers described above provide insufficient means to respond effectively and speedily to unlawful or illegal occupation of land. A straightforward and speedy remedy is needed.

> There is the basic problem that travellers evicted from one site may simply move to a nearby site, or to a site elsewhere in an authority's area, or just within the boundaries of an adjacent authority. In any case, such a measure does nothing to address the fundamental fact of the existence of significant numbers of travellers, and in effect has little real deterrent value, serving only to keep travellers on the move. (Association of District Councils)
>
> Local authority staff and police officers would, if all the proposals were adopted, find themselves forcing a caravan and its occupants off land, without being able to specify a legal site. (South Wales Constabulary)

Accordingly, it is proposed that:

i) it should be a criminal offence for any person to station a caravan for the purpose of residing for any period within England and Wales on any land situated within the boundaries of a highway, or any other unoccupied or common land, or any occupied land without the consent of the owner or tenant. (Where camping is *with consent*, but unlawful because in breach of planning controls, the law has recently been strengthened (see paragraph 18 above) and the maximum penalty for failing to comply with a stop notice is now £20,000);

ii) a magistrate may, under expedited procedures on the complaint of the local or highway authority, issue a warrant (subject to reasonable safeguards and perhaps on a similar basis to the procedures for search warrants) authorising that authority to take such steps as may be specified in the warrant for the removal from land of caravans stationed in contravention of (i) above;

iii) a magistrates' court may, on the complaint of the local or highway authority, by order prohibit offenders from returning for the purpose set out in (i) above to within one (or more) mile(s) of any site from which they have been evicted for a period of two years.

After carefully weighing all the various factors and taking into account our experience of local authorities and of the gipsy population, the NFU has concluded that resolution of the problems identified in the paper would not be assisted by absolving local authorities from their present duty. Indeed, the difficulties for farmers could well be exacerbated if this course of action was implemented. (National Farmers Union)

There is resistance to the proposal to 'criminalise' the act of living in a caravan. It is felt to be a unique situation to proscribe a way of life, formerly accepted as being within the law and then to introduce penalties. Whilst recognising the problems, the Police do not have any great difficulty in 'policing' the gipsy and itinerant communities. The changes proposed would by definition cause many previously law abiding people to be outside the law and in consequence subject to its process. The resource implications for the Police and the courts might be extremely high at a time when the resources are needed for other pressing demands. (General Purposes Committee, Association of Chief Police Officers (ACPO), on behalf of all Chief Constables, responding to a query from the National Romani Rights Association as to ACPO views on the changes)

21 Plainly it is important to ensure effective use of the proposed enhanced powers set out in paragraph 20 above. The penalty for obstructing or resisting eviction under warrant or for failing to comply with the terms of a prohibition order, could be a fine. But fine enforcement by the courts against a moving population is very difficult and the last resort for fine default – imprisonment – may be reached in a high proportion of cases. An alternative penalty would be to seize the caravan; such action would also prevent the offence being repeated. The Government invites views on whether local and highway authorities should be empowered by magistrates' courts to seize caravans whose removal was obstructed or resisted, or which returned in breach of a prohibition order. Clearly such action could only be contemplated as a last resort, when the law was being flouted, and if it were feasible and operationally practicable. The seized caravans would be returned when the offender(s) satisfied the court that he (they) either had a legal place to camp or alternative accommodation.

Local authority staff and police officers would, if all the proposals were adopted, find themselves forcing a caravan and its occupants off land, without being able to specify a legal site. The proposal to seize caravans as a means of fine enforcement is full of inherent problems, there being no indications as to who will be responsible for the "seizure" and storage of the seized caravans. (Chief Constable, South Wales Constabulary)

[A]ll caravans should be registered and carry their identifying national number. This would be in addition to the obligation to carry the number of the vehicle which is towing the caravan. In addition to the obvious advantage of identification of a caravan for enforcement of caravan law there would be some additional advantages in other areas of law enforcement. (National Association of Local Councils)

Accommodation for Gypsies and other Travellers

22 The number of caravans on private gypsy sites in England and Wales has increased by 114% from 1,400 in 1981 to nearly 3,000; while caravans on local authority sites have gone up 56% from about 3,800 to nearly 6,000 over the same period. At present, 100% grant is available towards the capital costs, including refurbishment, of local authority sites, but no assistance is given for day-to-day running costs.

[W]e would point out that a financial subsidy for accommodation costs is not confined to gypsies. Very substantial public subsidy of housing is given through public housing rents, mortgage interest relief, housing benefit and subsidies to housing associations. Put in this context, we wonder whether there is such privilege in practice. (JUSTICE (the British Section of the International Commission of Jurists))

23 People who wish to adopt a nomadic existence should be free to do so, provided they live within the law in the same way as their fellow citizens. This choice should not, however, entail a privileged position under the law or an entitlement to a greater degree of support from the taxpayer than is made available to those who choose a more settled existence. Travellers, like other citizens, should seek to provide their own accommodation, seeking planning permission where necessary like anyone else.

It is evident that the proposals will prevent that choice being exercised because of the lack of authorised sites and that is unlikely to change. (Wiltshire County Council)

Gypsies have, in general, a number of fine qualities including their strong family ties and self-reliance. In general they are a group of people who would not normally look to state subsidy; normally independent and able to fend for themselves. Given an even playing field for planning permissions they would almost certainly accommodate themselves. (Thorpes Solicitors, Hereford)

Our experience is that Gypsies and Travellers far from being 'privileged' are often discriminated against. They frequently find it hard to get help under Part III of the Housing Act 1985 as they do not have the same level of proof of identity as settled citizens. That many Travellers are illiterate serves to exacerbate this problem. Travellers suffer similar discrimination at the Department of Social Security and are not entitled to the same benefits as most of the rest of the community because they are treated as having no fixed abode. They are expected to pay Community Charge although less is provided for them than other members of the community. Under the Community Charge Regulations a distress warrant can be enforced against them for goods and chattels. A house cannot be counted as goods or chattels, but a caravan can. (SHAC (The London Housing Aid Centre))

This ignores the fact that many Travellers do not "adopt" a nomadic lifestyle but that they are born into it. It also disregards the fact that in reality the proposals in the Paper would marginalise the Travellers even further. If the Government has failed to achieve adequate site provision within a legal framework, it can hardly be expected that Travellers themselves will be able to do so without legislation to assist them. (Safe Childbirth for Travellers Campaign)

Repeal of 1968 duties

24 Accordingly, the Government proposes that the demand for local authority sites should be lessened by:

a) repealing the 1968 Act provisions which put a duty on local authorities to provide sites. Instead, local authorities would be given a discretionary power to provide sites where they believe this is the appropriate course to take. Caravan sites may be the most effective way of securing accommodation for travellers whom an authority accepts as statutorily homeless under Part III of the Housing Act 1985;

b) repealing the Secretary of State's powers to designate and to direct local authorities; and

c) encouraging gypsies who have settled in an area to move from caravan sites into both private and public sector housing.

The Government expects existing caravan sites to continue in being not least because, where grant has been paid towards the capital costs of a site, local authorities would have both to repay grant if the site closes and to provide alternative accommodation for any people from the site whom they accept as statutorily homeless.

[T]he proposal to remove the present "designation" process is a slight to such authorities as this Council who have responded in a responsible way to the needs of travelling people by ensuring the continued provision of a gypsy caravan site. (Nuneaton and Bedworth Borough Council)

The Trust believes that the repeal of the 1968 Act provisions, and the granting of discretionary powers in their stead, will result in a lack of incentive for local authorities to provide sites. It is arguable that local authorities which have not the commitment to discharge a statutory obligation are unlikely to execute this responsibility under a discretionary power. (The National Trust)

Exchequer grant

25 The Secretaries of State intend to adopt a fresh policy to guide the payment of 100% grant for the capital costs of sites (which has cost the Exchequer over £56 million since it became available in July 1978), namely that it should cease to be payable generally. A letter is being sent today to every local authority, setting out the factors which the Secretaries of State will take into account in considering future applications for grant from authorities.

Encouragement towards settlement and permanent housing

26 There is evidence that some gypsy and travelling families who have historically been travellers now prefer a more settled existence. As indicated in paragraph 9 above, gypsies have become progressively more settled, but people who have been nomadic may find transfer into traditional housing difficult. It may only be achieved by a transitional process – from temporary site, to permanent site, and then to carefully selected housing – over a period of years. Some caravan sites have experienced management problems; too hasty a transition into housing could result in those problems being transferred as well.

NALC warmly welcomes the proposals in paragraphs 26 to 28 of the consultation paper for policies to encourage permanent settlement of gypsies and a greater readiness of the settled population to accept such permanent settlements. (National Association of Local Councils (NALC))

The proposed policy of encouraging gipsies to move into permanent housing was applied by the former communist regimes in Eastern Europe and widely condemned for what it was, namely an attempt to destroy the identity of a national minority. Given the shortage of public housing, it would increase anti-gipsy prejudice among those at present on housing waiting lists. Indeed one consequence of the Eastern European policy has been increased and continuing prejudice against gipsies. (Liberal Democrat Lawyers)

27 Moreover, proposals for official gypsy sites, whether provided by local authorities or by the private sector, often encounter opposition because of local communities' experience of illegal camping. This means that gypsies may not find it easy to provide sites for themselves and, if they do manage to find a site, the process of settling down and possibly transferring into traditional housing may not be easy for people who are accustomed to a nomadic life-style. Accordingly, the Government believes that it may be necessary to provide advice on education, health and housing which encourages gypsies and other travellers to settle and, in time, to transfer into traditional housing. It may also be necessary to inform public opinion about the advantages of permitting official sites and encouraging gypsies to settle so that they become integrated into the community.

Such help as the consultation paper does propose to these groups has a distasteful air of social engineering. (Social Responsibility Department, Southwark Diocese)

This has significant implications for Travellers, both in relation to their civil rights and in relation to reinforcing negative stereotypes in public attitudes about them ... the emphasis on movement into permanent housing, especially the use of the term "carefully selected housing" (Para. 26), is seen as threatening in view of its historical association with the compulsory rehousing of Travellers prior to their arrest and transfer to concentration camps in Hitler's Third Reich. (The Law Centres Federation)

28 The Government is also considering whether it might be feasible to introduce a limited form of financial assistance towards the purchase of permanent housing for gypsies who vacate pitches on publicly-owned caravan sites, similar to the scheme for council tenants who wish to purchase a private property. To facilitate educational opportunities for traveller children, priority for vacancies then arising on existing public authorised sites might be given to travellers with children of compulsory school age.

The matter is further complicated by possible interpretations of 'intentionality' and 'suitable alternative accommodation' for those made homeless by the seizure of caravans. What is 'suitable' for a person/family of a nomadic lifestyle?... The Institute would welcome the opportunity to assess evidence from any research which the Department may have commissioned to support the assertion that increasing numbers of gypsy and other travelling families 'now prefer a more settled existence'. (Institute of Housing)

The proposed "encouragement" of gypsy and travelling families towards settlement and permanent housing together with the suggested gradual transition towards "carefully selected housing", suggests implications which may well be unacceptable to this Council. (Name of respondent unknown. On the document itself are handwritten comments made by two civil servants: one asked whether the phrase "carefully selected housing" was indeed contained in the paper, and another wrote "Afraid so!")

Planning policy

29 Gypsies enjoy a privileged position in the planning system, in that Government advice (DoE Circular 28/77 (Welsh Office Circular 51/77) and DoE Circular 57/78 (Welsh Office Circular 97/78)) recognises that in some circumstances it may be appropriate to countenance gypsy sites in the Green Belts, where normally the most restrictive regime applies. Since the Government proposes to remove local authorities' obligation to provide gypsy sites at public expense, it considers that the planning system should apply to gypsies on the same terms as anyone else. It proposes to up-date the relevant planning guidance to local authorities, to reflect the reform proposals that emerge from this consultation. Unlike gypsies, *travelling showpeople* do not enjoy a privileged position in the planning system and are subject to the same controls as other small businesses and self-employed people. Advice to local authorities about planning considerations relating to travelling showpeople is given in Circular 22/91.

The Committee has also expressed concern about the adequacies of the existing planning legislation both in respect of the granting of planning consent for Gypsy Sites and the enforcement of breaches of such legislation. It believes that a larger body other than current district councils would be more likely to give a balanced and objective view of such planning applications. (Suffolk County Council; next to this remark a civil servant has handwritten "Ho ho")

The Government must realise that green belt and similar land are the only really practical places for Gypsies to set up private sites. Other people are treated favourably in green belt areas with regard to planning permission, including Showmen, and the most favoured group of all being Farmers. (Essex Romani Association)

Many local authorities have made no provision whatsoever under the 1968 Act, citing as a reason for their inaction the pressure of their electors. Why does the DoE suppose that local authorities would be any more willing to grant planning permissions for sites owned and run by gipsies than they were to provide sites owned and managed by themselves? If the Department is going to go down this route, then it will have to adopt a firm policy of calling in planning applications for such sites in order to ensure that they are determined on planning grounds alone and not merely in response to local prejudice. (The Association of Landowning Charities)

Conclusions

30 The Government recognises that the proposals in this consultation paper represent a significant shift of policy. The changes proposed are justified, in the Government's view, because the present arrangements are satisfactory neither for local authorities, for local communities, for landowners, nor for gypsies and travellers. The public resents the unlawful or illegal occupation of land however it arises; and the 1968 Act duty to provide caravan sites is too loosely defined and has become an open-ended commitment, and a relentless drain on taxpayers' funds, undermining gypsies' responsibility to provide for themselves.

31 Accordingly, the Government believes that the proposals in this paper are a better way forward. They offer:

- swifter action to deal with illegal camping by those who persist in flouting the law;
- encouragement to all travellers to provide their own sites;
- more places on existing sites as some families move into permanent housing;
- and improved access to educational opportunities for travellers and their children.

If the County Councils cannot [provide sites] with all their financial resources and planning expertise, how on earth can private individuals be expected to cope with the system? (Mr W. Redman, Basingstoke)

It has been [our] experience that permanent sites do not encourage gypsies to settle in permanent housing. (The National Trust)

32 The Government invites views on the proposals for reform set out in this
   paper....

The paper offers no more convincing explanation of where on earth they will go and
we had better get wise to this if we are going to defend this policy. (Handwritten note
by a civil servant on a memorandum regarding the Wiltshire County Council response,
29 September 1992)

Appendix E: Racial attitudes and prejudice in Northern Ireland

Percentage of respondents unwilling to accept or mix with other ethnic groups

"I would not willingly accept the following person as ...	African Caribbean	Chinese	Irish Traveller	Member of other main religious tradition
... citizens of Northern Ireland who have come to live and work here"	18	16	45	10
... residents in my local area"	26	25	57	15
... a colleague at my work"	35	34	66	19
... a close friend of mine"	42	41	70	26
... a relative by way of marrying a close member of my family"	54	53	77	39

Source: Adapted from Connolly and Keenan (2000, p 18, Table 3.1)

Appendix F: Best Value and unauthorised encampments in Dorset

The following dialogue is from a question and answer session with David Ayre, Environmental Services, Dorset County Council, July 2000 TLRU seminar (see p 83).

Can traditional stopping places such as Shaftesbury Common be considered 'services' in Best Value terms?

> Lack or removal of them costs money, so 'economy, efficiency and effectiveness' as proscribed by Best Value are very much an issue.

It is clear that Dorset have undertaken a quasi-Best Value review of Traveller-related services. Where therefore is the 'compete' element?

> This is difficult: in some ways the Council is competing with itself, and also with Government guidance and research as it comes out. And some elements of managing unauthorised encampments involve a competitive element, such as the use and choice of contractors.

Surely encampments do not fit comfortably as a Best Value issue?

> The last Government surely thought so since they used the cost of site provision (£56 million over 24 years) as a justification to remove the duty to provide them. It may of course depend on an authority's policy statement as mentioned previously, but you cannot know whether something is 'cost effective' unless you know the costs and can identify the means and ends of a policy (or the lack of a policy).

How do you obtain the cooperation of other authorities such as districts for such a policy as that operated by Dorset County Council?

> District councils are happy to be co-operative when the County largely undertakes the work. Inter-agency working at all levels also helps, so that all involved understand the policies and processes at work.

Were targets and outcomes set as part of Dorset's programme?

> No, as this was before Best Value came in. It is difficult to identify quantitative measures anyway, aside from savings, as the number of unauthorised

encampments is not always predictable and may depend upon the action (or inaction) of other local authority areas.

Could meaningful performance indicators in this area include reduction in the costs of cleaning encampments, or in staff costs of dealing with complaints?

Absolutely, either because toleration means there are less encampments overall and/or because of improved liaison, negotiation and relationships with the residents of encampments and the public generally. There may also be 'positive' measures such as improved educational attainment by Travellers, or improvements in sustainability programmes and targets of authorities. Objectives can be realistically set in relation to these examples. Local action may in time improve the Best Value of policies set at the national level.

Appendix G: Northampton Borough Council *Best Value review of encampments*

The Best Value review of encampments examines the council's activity with regards to unauthorised encampments and aims to identify how economic and efficient the service is and to discover to what extent it meets the needs of its stakeholders.

The service has strong links with the community and requires close working with other partner agencies.

There is no mandatory duty on the local authority to provide sites for Travellers or to evict encampments. However, Northampton Borough Council, in line with relevant legislation and Home Office guidance, does take on the responsibility for Travellers in its area and is keen to develop a strategy which allows both the settled community and the Traveller community to live together within its borough.

The Best Value review team were of the opinion that currently officers do provide a good service with respect to unauthorised encampments. The council has had considerable success in reducing the numbers of unauthorised encampments over the last three years and the number of complaints has fallen. Northampton Borough Council is already recognised as an example of good practice by the Department of Environment, Transport and the Regions and the multi-agency working and the protocols agreed with the police are evidence of the efforts which has been focussed [sic] on Traveller issues in recent years.

It is recognised, however, that the current situation in Northampton is unsatisfactory. The cost of continually moving on encampments is borne by the local authority, residents, businesses and the Travellers. Unauthorised encampments receive high profile attention from the media and provoke a strong public and political reaction.

What does seem clear to the review team is that Best Value does not support the non-toleration of unauthorised encampments. The costs of eviction will continue to rise if alternatives to the cycle of evictions within the town are not pursued.

In carrying out the review, the review team have looked at the four Cs – challenge, compare, consult, compete. A large proportion of the review period was focused on the consultation element and a considerable amount of feedback was obtained from a wide range of stakeholders regarding the current service and ways in which improvements could be made.

Summary of recommendations

From observations evidenced throughout the review, the review team have concluded a series of recommendations [which] ... can be summarised into the following key areas:

Site provision

- The council should proceed with the identification of Family Allocated sites and should consult further with residents, business and Travellers regarding allocation, management policy and provision of facilities.
- A variety of site provision is required within the borough, which should be part of a wider network of site provision both on a county and national basis.

Organisation

- Consideration needs to be given to the separation of the enforcement and welfare roles of dealing with unauthorised encampments.
- The setting up of a multi-disciplinary Traveller Team should be investigated.
- A more corporate responsibility for Traveller issues is desirable.

Communication

- There is a need to review communication functions both internally and externally with regards to wider accessibility of public information, improved communication with Travellers and developing a proactive public relations/ media strategy.

Customer care

- Improvements are required to provide a more customer-focused service which can be achieved through the greater use of information technology, training and designated responsibilities.

An essential requirement is that the results of the consultation exercise and outcome of the Best Value review is effectively communicated to the public and to the other stakeholders who took part in the review.

An action plan detailing all the recommendation(s) will provide the basis for securing improvements to the service and this needs to be monitored and reviewed on a regular basis by members and officers.

(Northampton Borough Council, 2001, Executive Summary)

Appendix H: DETR and Audit Commission 2000/01 Best Value Performance Indicators relating to race equality issues

1. Introduction

There are at least 29 performance indicators that relate to racial equality issues in this year's DETR/Audit Commission's set of performance indicators. The LARRIE (Local Authority Race Relations Information Exchange) database holds many examples of local authorities that have developed policies and practices for responding to these indicators, ranging from adoption of the CRE Standard to using the 2001 Census ethnic group categories to monitor recruitment and selection.

For further information please send an e-mail to (author of this briefing note) sarah.palmer@lg-employers.gov.uk or ring 020 7296 6779.

2. Performance indicators

2.1. Corporate health BVPIs

BVPI2: The level of the Commission for Racial Equality's 'Standard for Local Government' to which the authority conforms.
Definition: This performance indicator refers to the provision of services to the community.
BVPI3: The percentage of citizens satisfied with the overall service provided by their authority.
Definition: See section 3 for survey requirements.
BVPI4: The percentage of those making complaints satisfied with the handling of those complaints.
Definition: See section 3 for survey requirements.
BVPI17: Minority ethnic community staff as a percentage of the total workforce.
Definition: Local authorities should use the 2001 Census ethnicity categories and include staff in schools.

2.2. Police authority corporate health PIs

BVPI25: The percentage of minority ethnic community police staff in the force and the percentage of minority ethnic community population of working age in the force area.

Definition: 'Minority ethnic population of working age' is based on persons aged 18-54, from the Labour Force Survey (1996-98 12 quarters – as published by the Home Office on 28 July 1999 in *Race equality – the Home Secretary's employment targets* published under section 95 of the 1991 Criminal Justice Act).

2.3. Single-service fire authority corporate health PIs

BVPI2: The level of the Commission for Racial Equality's 'Standard for Local Government' to which the authority conforms.

Definition: This performance indicator refers to the provision of services to the community.

BVPI3: The percentage of citizens satisfied with the overall service provided by their authority.

BVPI4: The percentage of those making complaints satisfied with the handling of those complaints.

BVPI17: The percentage of minority ethnic community uniformed staff and the percentage of minority ethnic community population of working age in the brigade area.

2.4. National parks and national Broad authority corporate health PIs

BVPI2: The level of the Commission for Racial Equality's 'Standard for Local Government' to which the authority conforms.

Definition: This performance indicator refers to the provision of services to the community.

BVPI17: Minority ethnic community staff as a percentage of the total workforce.

Definition: The 2001 Census categories should be used.

2.5. Joint waste disposal authority corporate health PIs

BVPI3: The percentage of citizens satisfied with the overall service provided by their authority.

BVPI4: The percentage of those making complaints satisfied with the handling of those complaints.

BVPI17: Minority ethnic communities staff as a percentage of the total workforce.
Definition: The 2001 Census categories should be used.

2.6. Corporate health audit commission PIs

AC-A2a: The number of racial incidents recorded by the authority per 100,000 population.
Definition: Racial incidents are any incidents regarded as such by the victim or anyone else. The indicator applies to all authority services (including schools) and racial incidents reported by employees of the authority.
AC-A2b: The percentage of racial incidents that resulted in further action.
Definition: Further action must be recorded in writing and would entail such things as:
Detailed investigations, for example interviews with alleged perpetrator(s)
Referral to the police or other body (CRE, CABs, etc)
Mediation
Warning to the perpetrator, which if oral must be recorded at the time
Relocation of the victim
Removal of graffiti.

2.7. Social services

BVPI60: Users/carers who said that matters relating to race, culture or religion were noted.
Definition: The percentage of people surveyed who said that they felt that matters relating to race, culture or religion were taken into account by social services in the provision of the help they needed. This will be obtained from user satisfaction surveys to be carried out by local authorities. Detailed guidance on sampling and survey methodology to be issued early in 2000.

2.8. Housing and related services

BVPI74: Satisfaction of tenants of council housing with the overall service provided by their landlord.
Definition: See section 3 for survey requirements.
BVPI75: Satisfaction of tenants of council housing with opportunities for participation in management and decision making in relation to housing service provided by their landlord.
Definition: See section 3 for survey requirements.
BVPI80: User satisfaction survey covering issues of accessibility, staffing issues (helpfulness, etc) and communications/information (understandability, etc).
Definition: See section 3 for survey requirements.

AC-D1: Does the authority follow the Commission for Racial Equality's code of practice in rented housing?
Definition: 'Following the code' must include adherence to all the code's recommendations except those relating to employment practices, including procedures for dealing with racial harassment and reporting the results of ethnic monitoring to a committee of the council.

2.9. Environmental services

BVPI89: Percentage of people satisfied with cleanliness standards.
Definition: See section 3 for survey requirements.
BVPI90: Percentage of people expressing satisfaction with a) recycling facilities, b) household water collection and c) civic amenities sites.
Definition: See section 3 for survey requirements.

2.10. Transport

BVPI103: Percentage of users satisfied with local provision of public transport information.
Definition: See section 3 for survey requirements.
BVPI104: Percentage of users satisfied with local bus services.
Definition: See section 3 for survey requirements.

2.11. Planning

BVPI112: Score against a checklist of planning practice (fair access).
Definition: Have you implemented a policy for ensuring that different groups have equal access to the planning process including, as necessary, the provision of advice in ethnic minority languages and in Braille/on tape, based on consultation with relevant members of the community about the accessibility of the planning service, and do you have arrangements for keeping this policy under review? Note authorities should consider how accessible the service they provide is to different groups in the population such as ethnic minorities, religious groups, elderly and disabled people and disadvantaged and deprived people in inner urban areas.

2.12. Cultural and related services

BVPI119: Percentage of residents by targeted group satisfied with the local authority's cultural and recreational activities.

Definition: Percentage of minority ethnic community respondents fairly satisfied or very satisfied with cultural and recreational facilities and activities. Definition: See section 3 for survey requirements.

2.13. Emergency services

BVPI139: Number of PACE stop/searches of minority ethnic persons per 1,000 minority ethnic population and percentage leading to arrest.
BVPI141: Percentage of reported racist incidents where further investigative action is taken and percentage of reported racially aggravated crimes detected. Definitions: 'Further investigative action' means where action is taken in addition to mere recording of initial attendance (excluding dispatch of leaflet or telephone contact). Further guidance will be issued in due course. 'Incident' means verbal abuse, threatening behaviour, graffiti, damage to property, physical attack, arson, murder. 'Racist incident' is any incident which is perceived to be racist by the victim or any other person.

3. Survey requirements

A number of the performance indicators listed previously indicate the need for an ethnicity category in user satisfaction surveys. The performance indicator document gives guidance on the conduct of surveys, covering desired sample size, the sampling method and the specific questions to be asked. It emphasises that all surveys will be required to contain questions on gender, age, occupation, employment status, disability and ethnicity, to facilitate comparability across authorities.

The document explains that estimates for subgroups of the population – including ethnic subgroups – are desirable because they will allow authorities to examine the impact of service provision on the subgroups. However, because the size of different subgroups will vary among authorities, the guidance does not prescribe a specific sample size for subgroups.

4. 2001 Census

The recommended question for gathering data on ethnicity is that to be used in the 2001 Census for England and Wales. This asks: to which of these groups do you consider you belong?
It offers the following categories:

White:
  British
  Irish
  Any other White background

Mixed:
  White and Black Caribbean
  White and Black African
  White and Asian
  Any other mixed background

Asian or Asian British:
  Indian
  Pakistani
  Bangladeshi
  Any other Asian background

Black or Black British:
  Caribbean
  African
  Any other Black background

Chinese or other ethnic group:
  Chinese
  Other

Reprinted with permission of Sarah Palmer
(Local Government Employers' Organisation for 2000)

Index

Also available from The Policy Press

Making a living
Social security, social exclusion and New Travellers
Lyn Webster and Jane Millar, Department of Social and Policy Sciences, University of Bath

To combat social exclusion the government has introduced a number of welfare reforms with the central aim of integrating people who can, and 'should', work into the labour market. This study explores the ways in which the marginalised and controversial New Traveller community participates in the labour market.

By focusing on the experiences of New Travellers, the report explores their patterns of paid work, benefit receipt and other sources of support, including that of community. In so doing, it provides insights into how New Travellers make a living and challenges the commonly held assumption that New Travellers are entirely dependent on the state.

This report will be of interest to all those engaged in the policy process, as well as academics and social policy students.

Paperback £10.95 ISBN 1 86134 331 0
297 x 210mm 48 pages May 2001 REPORT
Published in association with the Joseph Rowntree Foundation

Gypsies, Travellers and the Health Service
A study in inequality
Derek Hawes, formerly at the School for Policy Studies, University of Bristol

This report considers the relative poor health of nomadic families compared with settled peoples in England and Wales. It examines the effectiveness of the delivery of healthcare services to both traditional and 'new' travelling families, with particular reference to the quality of inter-professional and inter-agency collaboration.

Paperback £10.95 ISBN 1 86134 066 4
234 x 156mm 56 pages September 1997

MORE ▶

A directory of planning policies for Gypsy site provision in England

Mark Wilson, Woking Borough Council
Preface by Derek Hawes

One third of the Gypsy population have nowhere legal to stay. There is, therefore, a serious need for local authorities to change their policies and practices to allow Gypsies to secure accommodation in appropriate places. This is the only comprehensive survey ever carried out looking at this under-researched area of planning policy.

Paperback £29.99 ISBN 1 86134 082 6

297 x 210mm 280 pages April 1998 GUIDE

For further information about these and other titles published by The Policy Press, please visit our website at: www.policypress.org.uk or telephone +44 (0)117 954 6800

To order, please contact:
Marston Book Services
PO Box 269
Abingdon
Oxon OX14 4YN
UK
Tel: +44 (0)1235 465500
Fax: +44 (0)1235 465556
E-mail: direct.orders@marston.co.uk

The POLICY

P~P

PRESS